HEALTHY SOUPS: READY TO EAT LOW SODIUM COOKBOOK

Welcome To

These 100+ recipes blend traditional ingredients with healthy soups ready to eat low sodium

HEALTHY SOUPS

FOOD REGIMEN TO REFRESH YOUR HEALTHY SOUPS, THE ODYSSEY BOOK OF QUICK & EASY RECIPES, A COLLECTION OF MOUTHWATERING RECIPES AND CULINARY INSPIRATION.

By : Ani Janell

For any inquiries or questions regarding our books,

Please contact us at: anijanell77@gmail.com

ISBN: 9798327935273

Table of content

INTRODUCTION

"Healthy Soups: Ready to Eat Low Sodium Cookbook" is a culinary guide dedicated to the art of creating delicious, nutritious soups that are low in sodium. This cookbook caters to individuals who are health-conscious, particularly those who need or wish to reduce their salt intake without sacrificing flavor. Here's a detailed description:

Overview:

The cookbook offers a collection of soup recipes that emphasize the use of fresh, wholesome ingredients while minimizing sodium content. It is ideal for those managing hypertension, heart disease, or kidney issues, as well as anyone looking to maintain a balanced diet.

Key Features:

- **Variety of Recipes**: Includes a diverse array of soups, from classic comfort foods to innovative, exotic flavors, ensuring there is something for everyone.
- **Nutritional Information**: Each recipe comes with detailed nutritional information, focusing on sodium content, to help readers make informed dietary choices.
- **Easy-to-Follow Instructions**: The recipes are written in a clear, concise manner, making them accessible to both novice and experienced cooks.
- **Preparation Tips**: Offers practical tips on selecting low-sodium ingredients, as well as techniques to enhance flavor without adding salt.
- **Health Benefits**: Highlights the health benefits of various ingredients used in the recipes, promoting a holistic approach to wellness.
- **Ready-to-Eat Options**: Some recipes are designed for quick preparation, perfect for busy individuals who need healthy meals on the go.

Content Breakdown:

1. **Introduction**: An overview of the importance of a low-sodium diet and tips on how to transition to such a diet without compromising taste.
2. **Basic Techniques**: Covers the essentials of soup-making, including stock preparation, seasoning alternatives, and methods to build flavor.
3. **Soup Categories**:
    - **Vegetable Soups**: Focuses on soups rich in vegetables, offering nutrient-dense options.
    - **Bean and Legume Soups**: Provides hearty, protein-packed soups that are filling and nutritious.
    - **Grain Soups**: Features soups incorporating healthy grains like quinoa, barley, and rice.
    - **Protein Soups**: Includes recipes that use lean meats and seafood in low-sodium broths.
    - **Special Diet Soups**: Caters to specific dietary needs, such as vegan, gluten-free, and paleo-friendly soups.

4. **Seasonal Soups**: Recipes that utilize seasonal produce, ensuring fresh and flavorful dishes year-round.
5. **Garnishes and Add-ins**: Suggestions for low-sodium garnishes and add-ins to enhance the final presentation and taste of the soups.

Conclusion:

The "Healthy Soups: Ready to Eat Low Sodium Cookbook" is a valuable resource for anyone looking to enjoy delicious soups while maintaining a low-sodium diet. It combines practical culinary advice with a variety of flavorful recipes, making healthy eating both enjoyable and sustainable.

1. HEARTY LENTIL SOUP

Ingredients:

- 1 cup lentils, rinsed
- 1 large onion, chopped
- 2 carrots, chopped
- 2 celery stalks, chopped
- 3 cloves garlic, minced
- 1 can diced tomatoes (no salt added)
- 6 cups low-sodium vegetable broth
- 1 tsp cumin
- 1 tsp smoked paprika
- 1 bay leaf
- Salt and pepper to taste
- 2 tbsp olive oil
- 2 cups spinach, chopped

Instructions:

1. Heat olive oil in a large pot over medium heat. Add onion, carrots, and celery. Sauté until softened, about 5 minutes.

2. Add garlic, cumin, and smoked paprika. Cook for another minute.
3. Stir in lentils, tomatoes, broth, and bay leaf. Bring to a boil.
4. Reduce heat, cover, and simmer for 30-35 minutes until lentils are tender.
5. Remove bay leaf, stir in spinach, and cook until wilted. Season with salt and pepper.
6. Serve hot.

2. CHICKEN AND VEGETABLE SOUP

Ingredients:

- 2 boneless, skinless chicken breasts, cubed
- 1 large onion, chopped
- 3 carrots, sliced
- 3 celery stalks, sliced
- 3 cloves garlic, minced
- 6 cups low-sodium chicken broth
- 1 tsp dried thyme
- 1 tsp dried rosemary
- 1 bay leaf
- 1 cup green beans, trimmed and cut into 1-inch pieces
- 1 cup peas
- 2 tbsp olive oil
- Salt and pepper to taste

Instructions:

1. Heat olive oil in a large pot over medium heat. Add onion, carrots, and celery. Sauté until vegetables are tender, about 5-7 minutes.
2. Add garlic and cook for another minute.
3. Stir in chicken, broth, thyme, rosemary, and bay leaf. Bring to a boil.
4. Reduce heat and simmer for 20 minutes, until chicken is cooked through.

5. Add green beans and peas, cooking until tender, about 5 minutes.
6. Season with salt and pepper. Remove bay leaf before serving.
7. Serve hot.

3. TOMATO BASIL SOUP

Ingredients:

- 2 tbsp olive oil
- 1 large onion, chopped
- 3 cloves garlic, minced
- 2 cans (28 oz each) no-salt-added whole tomatoes
- 4 cups low-sodium vegetable broth
- 1 tsp sugar
- 1/2 cup fresh basil leaves, chopped
- 1 cup low-fat milk or almond milk
- Salt and pepper to taste

Instructions:

1. Heat olive oil in a large pot over medium heat. Add onion and cook until softened, about 5 minutes.
2. Add garlic and cook for another minute.
3. Stir in tomatoes (with juice) and broth. Bring to a boil.
4. Reduce heat and simmer for 20 minutes.
5. Use an immersion blender to puree the soup until smooth.
6. Stir in sugar, basil, and milk. Heat through without boiling.
7. Season with salt and pepper. Serve hot.

4. BUTTERNUT SQUASH SOUP

Ingredients:

- 1 large butternut squash, peeled, seeded, and cubed
- 2 tbsp olive oil
- 1 large onion, chopped

- 3 cloves garlic, minced
- 4 cups low-sodium vegetable broth
- 1 tsp ground nutmeg
- 1/2 cup coconut milk
- Salt and pepper to taste

Instructions:

1. Heat olive oil in a large pot over medium heat. Add onion and cook until softened, about 5 minutes.
2. Add garlic and cook for another minute.
3. Stir in butternut squash and broth. Bring to a boil.
4. Reduce heat and simmer for 20-25 minutes, until squash is tender.
5. Use an immersion blender to puree the soup until smooth.
6. Stir in nutmeg and coconut milk. Heat through without boiling.
7. Season with salt and pepper. Serve hot.

5. CARROT GINGER SOUP

Ingredients:

- 2 tbsp olive oil
- 1 large onion, chopped
- 3 cloves garlic, minced
- 1 tbsp fresh ginger, minced
- 6 large carrots, peeled and chopped
- 4 cups low-sodium vegetable broth
- 1/2 cup coconut milk
- Salt and pepper to taste

Instructions:

1. Heat olive oil in a large pot over medium heat. Add onion and cook until softened, about 5 minutes.
2. Add garlic and ginger, and cook for another minute.
3. Stir in carrots and broth. Bring to a boil.

4. Reduce heat and simmer for 20-25 minutes, until carrots are tender.
5. Use an immersion blender to puree the soup until smooth.
6. Stir in coconut milk. Heat through without boiling.
7. Season with salt and pepper. Serve hot.

6. SPINACH AND WHITE BEAN SOUP

Ingredients:

- 2 tbsp olive oil
- 1 large onion, chopped
- 3 cloves garlic, minced
- 4 cups low-sodium vegetable broth
- 2 cans (15 oz each) cannellini beans, drained and rinsed
- 4 cups fresh spinach, chopped
- 1 tsp dried thyme
- Salt and pepper to taste

Instructions:

1. Heat olive oil in a large pot over medium heat. Add onion and cook until softened, about 5 minutes.
2. Add garlic and cook for another minute.
3. Stir in broth, beans, and thyme. Bring to a boil.
4. Reduce heat and simmer for 10 minutes.
5. Add spinach and cook until wilted, about 5 minutes.
6. Season with salt and pepper. Serve hot.

7. SWEET POTATO AND BLACK BEAN SOUP

Ingredients:

- 2 tbsp olive oil
- 1 large onion, chopped

- 3 cloves garlic, minced
- 2 medium sweet potatoes, peeled and diced
- 4 cups low-sodium vegetable broth
- 1 can (15 oz) black beans, drained and rinsed
- 1 tsp cumin
- 1 tsp chili powder
- Salt and pepper to taste
- Juice of 1 lime

Instructions:

1. Heat olive oil in a large pot over medium heat. Add onion and cook until softened, about 5 minutes.
2. Add garlic, cumin, and chili powder. Cook for another minute.
3. Stir in sweet potatoes and broth. Bring to a boil.
4. Reduce heat and simmer for 20 minutes, until sweet potatoes are tender.
5. Stir in black beans and lime juice. Heat through.
6. Season with salt and pepper. Serve hot.

8. KALE AND QUINOA SOUP

Ingredients:

- 2 tbsp olive oil
- 1 large onion, chopped
- 3 cloves garlic, minced
- 1 cup quinoa, rinsed
- 6 cups low-sodium vegetable broth
- 4 cups chopped kale
- 1 can (15 oz) diced tomatoes (no salt added)
- 1 tsp dried thyme
- Salt and pepper to taste

Instructions:

1. Heat olive oil in a large pot over medium heat. Add onion and cook until softened, about 5 minutes.

2. Add garlic and cook for another minute.
3. Stir in quinoa, broth, tomatoes, and thyme. Bring to a boil.
4. Reduce heat and simmer for 15 minutes.
5. Add kale and cook until wilted, about 5 minutes.
6. Season with salt and pepper. Serve hot.

9. MUSHROOM BARLEY SOUP

Ingredients:

- 2 tbsp olive oil
- 1 large onion, chopped
- 3 cloves garlic, minced
- 2 cups sliced mushrooms
- 1 cup pearl barley
- 6 cups low-sodium vegetable broth
- 1 tsp dried thyme
- 1 bay leaf
- Salt and pepper to taste

Instructions:

1. Heat olive oil in a large pot over medium heat. Add onion and cook until softened, about 5 minutes.
2. Add garlic and mushrooms, and cook until mushrooms are browned, about 5-7 minutes.
3. Stir in barley, broth, thyme, and bay leaf. Bring to a boil.
4. Reduce heat and simmer for 40-45 minutes, until barley is tender.
5. Remove bay leaf. Season with salt and pepper. Serve hot.

10. CAULIFLOWER LEEK SOUP

Ingredients:

- 2 tbsp olive oil
- 2 leeks, white and light green parts only, chopped

- 3 cloves garlic, minced
- 1 large head of cauliflower, chopped
- 4 cups low-sodium vegetable broth
- 1/2 cup low-fat milk or almond milk
- Salt and pepper to taste

Instructions:

1. Heat olive oil in a large pot over medium heat. Add leeks and cook until softened, about 5 minutes.
2. Add garlic and cook for another minute.
3. Stir in cauliflower and broth. Bring to a boil.
4. Reduce heat and simmer for 20-25 minutes, until cauliflower is tender.
5. Use an immersion blender to puree the soup until smooth.
6. Stir in milk. Heat through without boiling.
7. Season with salt and pepper. Serve hot.

11. ZUCCHINI BASIL SOUP

Ingredients:

- 2 tbsp olive oil
- 1 large onion, chopped
- 3 cloves garlic, minced
- 4 medium zucchinis, chopped
- 4 cups low-sodium vegetable broth
- 1 cup fresh basil leaves, chopped
- 1/2 cup low-fat milk or almond milk
- Salt and pepper to taste

Instructions:

1. Heat olive oil in a large pot over medium heat. Add onion and cook until softened, about 5 minutes.
2. Add garlic and cook for another minute.
3. Stir in zucchinis and broth. Bring to a boil.

4. Reduce heat and simmer for 15-20 minutes, until zucchinis are tender.
5. Use an immersion blender to puree the soup until smooth.
6. Stir in basil and milk. Heat through without boiling.
7. Season with salt and pepper. Serve hot.

12. ROASTED RED PEPPER SOUP

Ingredients:

- 4 large red bell peppers
- 2 tbsp olive oil
- 1 large onion, chopped
- 3 cloves garlic, minced
- 4 cups low-sodium vegetable broth
- 1 tsp smoked paprika
- 1/2 cup coconut milk
- Salt and pepper to taste

Instructions:

1. Preheat the oven to 425°F (220°C). Place bell peppers on a baking sheet and roast for 25-30 minutes until skins are charred.
2. Place roasted peppers in a bowl and cover with plastic wrap for 10 minutes. Peel off the skins, remove seeds, and chop.
3. Heat olive oil in a large pot over medium heat. Add onion and cook until softened, about 5 minutes.
4. Add garlic and smoked paprika, and cook for another minute.
5. Stir in roasted peppers and broth. Bring to a boil.
6. Reduce heat and simmer for 15 minutes.
7. Use an immersion blender to puree the soup until smooth.
8. Stir in coconut milk. Heat through without boiling.
9. Season with salt and pepper. Serve hot.

13. BROCCOLI CHEDDAR SOUP

Ingredients:

- 2 tbsp olive oil
- 1 large onion, chopped
- 3 cloves garlic, minced
- 4 cups broccoli florets
- 4 cups low-sodium vegetable broth
- 1 cup shredded low-fat cheddar cheese
- 1/2 cup low-fat milk or almond milk
- Salt and pepper to taste

Instructions:

1. Heat olive oil in a large pot over medium heat. Add onion and cook until softened, about 5 minutes.
2. Add garlic and cook for another minute.
3. Stir in broccoli and broth. Bring to a boil.
4. Reduce heat and simmer for 15-20 minutes, until broccoli is tender.
5. Use an immersion blender to puree the soup until smooth.
6. Stir in cheddar cheese and milk. Heat through without boiling.
7. Season with salt and pepper. Serve hot.

14. PUMPKIN CURRY SOUP

Ingredients:

- 2 tbsp olive oil
- 1 large onion, chopped
- 3 cloves garlic, minced
- 1 tbsp fresh ginger, minced
- 4 cups pumpkin puree (canned or fresh)
- 4 cups low-sodium vegetable broth
- 1 can (15 oz) coconut milk
- 1 tbsp curry powder
- Salt and pepper to taste

Instructions:

1. Heat olive oil in a large pot over medium heat. Add onion and cook until softened, about 5 minutes.
2. Add garlic, ginger, and curry powder, and cook for another minute.
3. Stir in pumpkin puree and broth. Bring to a boil.
4. Reduce heat and simmer for 15 minutes.
5. Stir in coconut milk. Heat through without boiling.
6. Season with salt and pepper. Serve hot.

15. CHICKPEA AND SPINACH SOUP

Ingredients:

- 2 tbsp olive oil
- 1 large onion, chopped
- 3 cloves garlic, minced
- 1 can (15 oz) chickpeas, drained and rinsed
- 4 cups low-sodium vegetable broth
- 4 cups fresh spinach, chopped
- 1 tsp cumin
- 1 tsp smoked paprika
- Salt and pepper to taste

Instructions:

1. Heat olive oil in a large pot over medium heat. Add onion and cook until softened, about 5 minutes.
2. Add garlic, cumin, and smoked paprika. Cook for another minute.
3. Stir in chickpeas and broth. Bring to a boil.
4. Reduce heat and simmer for 10 minutes.
5. Add spinach and cook until wilted, about 5 minutes.
6. Season with salt and pepper. Serve hot.

16. ASPARAGUS AND PEA SOUP

Ingredients:

- 2 tbsp olive oil
- 1 large onion, chopped
- 3 cloves garlic, minced
- 1 bunch asparagus, trimmed and chopped
- 2 cups frozen peas
- 4 cups low-sodium vegetable broth
- 1/2 cup fresh mint leaves, chopped
- 1/2 cup low-fat milk or almond milk
- Salt and pepper to taste

Instructions:

1. Heat olive oil in a large pot over medium heat. Add onion and cook until softened, about 5 minutes.
2. Add garlic and cook for another minute.
3. Stir in asparagus and broth. Bring to a boil.
4. Reduce heat and simmer for 10-15 minutes, until asparagus is tender.
5. Add peas and cook for another 5 minutes.
6. Use an immersion blender to puree the soup until smooth.
7. Stir in mint and milk. Heat through without boiling.
8. Season with salt and pepper. Serve hot.

17. MINESTRONE SOUP

Ingredients:

- 2 tbsp olive oil
- 1 large onion, chopped
- 3 cloves garlic, minced
- 3 carrots, chopped
- 2 celery stalks, chopped
- 1 zucchini, chopped
- 1 cup green beans, trimmed and cut into 1-inch pieces
- 1 can (15 oz) diced tomatoes (no salt added)
- 6 cups low-sodium vegetable broth

- 1 can (15 oz) kidney beans, drained and rinsed
- 1 cup small pasta (e.g., ditalini)
- 1 tsp dried oregano
- 1 tsp dried basil
- 2 cups fresh spinach, chopped
- Salt and pepper to taste

Instructions:

1. Heat olive oil in a large pot over medium heat. Add onion, carrots, and celery. Cook until softened, about 5-7 minutes.
2. Add garlic, zucchini, and green beans. Cook for another 5 minutes.
3. Stir in tomatoes, broth, oregano, and basil. Bring to a boil.
4. Reduce heat and simmer for 15 minutes.
5. Add kidney beans and pasta. Cook until pasta is tender, about 10 minutes.
6. Stir in spinach and cook until wilted, about 2 minutes.
7. Season with salt and pepper. Serve hot.

18. CABBAGE AND SAUSAGE SOUP

Ingredients:

- 2 tbsp olive oil
- 1 large onion, chopped
- 3 cloves garlic, minced
- 1 lb turkey sausage, sliced
- 4 cups chopped cabbage
- 3 carrots, chopped
- 4 cups low-sodium chicken broth
- 1 can (15 oz) diced tomatoes (no salt added)
- 1 tsp dried thyme
- 1 tsp smoked paprika
- Salt and pepper to taste

Instructions:

1. Heat olive oil in a large pot over medium heat. Add onion and cook until softened, about 5 minutes.
2. Add garlic and sausage, cooking until sausage is browned, about 5 minutes.
3. Stir in cabbage, carrots, tomatoes, broth, thyme, and paprika. Bring to a boil.
4. Reduce heat and simmer for 20-25 minutes, until vegetables are tender.
5. Season with salt and pepper. Serve hot.

19. Green Pea Mint Soup

Ingredients:

- 2 tbsp olive oil
- 1 large onion, chopped
- 3 cloves garlic, minced
- 4 cups frozen peas
- 4 cups low-sodium vegetable broth
- 1/2 cup fresh mint leaves, chopped
- 1/2 cup low-fat milk or almond milk
- Salt and pepper to taste

Instructions:

1. Heat olive oil in a large pot over medium heat. Add onion and cook until softened, about 5 minutes.
2. Add garlic and cook for another minute.
3. Stir in peas and broth. Bring to a boil.
4. Reduce heat and simmer for 10 minutes.
5. Use an immersion blender to puree the soup until smooth.
6. Stir in mint and milk. Heat through without boiling.
7. Season with salt and pepper. Serve hot.

20. SPLIT PEA SOUP

Ingredients:

- 2 tbsp olive oil
- 1 large onion, chopped
- 3 cloves garlic, minced
- 2 carrots, chopped
- 2 celery stalks, chopped
- 2 cups dried split peas, rinsed
- 6 cups low-sodium vegetable broth
- 1 bay leaf
- 1 tsp dried thyme
- Salt and pepper to taste

Instructions:

1. Heat olive oil in a large pot over medium heat. Add onion, carrots, and celery. Cook until softened, about 5-7 minutes.
2. Add garlic and cook for another minute.
3. Stir in split peas, broth, bay leaf, and thyme. Bring to a boil.
4. Reduce heat and simmer for 1 hour, until peas are tender.
5. Remove bay leaf. Use an immersion blender to puree the soup until smooth, if desired.
6. Season with salt and pepper. Serve hot.

21. VEGETABLE BARLEY SOUP

Ingredients:

- 2 tbsp olive oil
- 1 large onion, chopped
- 3 cloves garlic, minced
- 2 carrots, chopped
- 2 celery stalks, chopped
- 1 zucchini, chopped
- 1 cup pearl barley
- 6 cups low-sodium vegetable broth
- 1 can (15 oz) diced tomatoes (no salt added)
- 1 tsp dried thyme
- 1 tsp dried oregano
- 2 cups fresh spinach, chopped

- Salt and pepper to taste

Instructions:

1. Heat olive oil in a large pot over medium heat. Add onion, carrots, and celery. Cook until softened, about 5-7 minutes.
2. Add garlic and cook for another minute.
3. Stir in zucchini, barley, broth, tomatoes, thyme, and oregano. Bring to a boil.
4. Reduce heat and simmer for 45 minutes, until barley is tender.
5. Stir in spinach and cook until wilted, about 2 minutes.
6. Season with salt and pepper. Serve hot.

22. POTATO LEEK SOUP

Ingredients:

- 2 tbsp olive oil
- 2 leeks, white and light green parts only, chopped
- 3 cloves garlic, minced
- 4 large potatoes, peeled and chopped
- 4 cups low-sodium vegetable broth
- 1 cup low-fat milk or almond milk
- 1 tsp dried thyme
- Salt and pepper to taste

Instructions:

1. Heat olive oil in a large pot over medium heat. Add leeks and cook until softened, about 5 minutes.
2. Add garlic and cook for another minute.
3. Stir in potatoes, broth, and thyme. Bring to a boil.
4. Reduce heat and simmer for 20-25 minutes, until potatoes are tender.
5. Use an immersion blender to puree the soup until smooth.
6. Stir in milk. Heat through without boiling.
7. Season with salt and pepper. Serve hot.

23. CORN AND POTATO CHOWDER

Ingredients:

- 2 tbsp olive oil
- 1 large onion, chopped
- 3 cloves garlic, minced
- 4 large potatoes, peeled and chopped
- 4 cups corn kernels (fresh or frozen)
- 4 cups low-sodium vegetable broth
- 1 cup low-fat milk or almond milk
- 1 tsp dried thyme
- Salt and pepper to taste

Instructions:

1. Heat olive oil in a large pot over medium heat. Add onion and cook until softened, about 5 minutes.
2. Add garlic and cook for another minute.
3. Stir in potatoes, corn, broth, and thyme. Bring to a boil.
4. Reduce heat and simmer for 20-25 minutes, until potatoes are tender.
5. Use an immersion blender to puree the soup to your desired consistency.
6. Stir in milk. Heat through without boiling.
7. Season with salt and pepper. Serve hot.

24. CARROT CORIANDER SOUP

Ingredients:

- 2 tbsp olive oil
- 1 large onion, chopped
- 3 cloves garlic, minced
- 6 large carrots, peeled and chopped
- 4 cups low-sodium vegetable broth
- 1 tsp ground coriander

- 1/2 cup low-fat milk or almond milk
- Salt and pepper to taste

Instructions:

1. Heat olive oil in a large pot over medium heat. Add onion and cook until softened, about 5 minutes.
2. Add garlic and coriander, and cook for another minute.
3. Stir in carrots and broth. Bring to a boil.
4. Reduce heat and simmer for 20-25 minutes, until carrots are tender.
5. Use an immersion blender to puree the soup until smooth.
6. Stir in milk. Heat through without boiling.
7. Season with salt and pepper. Serve hot.

25. FENNEL AND APPLE SOUP

Ingredients:

- 2 tbsp olive oil
- 1 large onion, chopped
- 2 bulbs fennel, trimmed and chopped
- 3 cloves garlic, minced
- 3 large apples, peeled and chopped
- 4 cups low-sodium vegetable broth
- 1/2 cup low-fat milk or almond milk
- Salt and pepper to taste

Instructions:

1. Heat olive oil in a large pot over medium heat. Add onion and fennel. Cook until softened, about 5-7 minutes.
2. Add garlic and cook for another minute.
3. Stir in apples and broth. Bring to a boil.
4. Reduce heat and simmer for 20-25 minutes, until apples and fennel are tender.
5. Use an immersion blender to puree the soup until smooth.
6. Stir in milk. Heat through without boiling.

7. Season with salt and pepper. Serve hot.

26. COCONUT CURRY SOUP

Ingredients:

- 2 tbsp coconut oil
- 1 large onion, chopped
- 3 cloves garlic, minced
- 1 tbsp fresh ginger, minced
- 2 tbsp red curry paste
- 4 cups low-sodium vegetable broth
- 1 can (15 oz) coconut milk
- 1 cup carrots, sliced
- 1 cup bell peppers, sliced
- 1 cup snow peas
- Juice of 1 lime
- Salt and pepper to taste

Instructions:

1. Heat coconut oil in a large pot over medium heat. Add onion and cook until softened, about 5 minutes.
2. Add garlic, ginger, and curry paste, and cook for another minute.
3. Stir in broth, coconut milk, carrots, and bell peppers. Bring to a boil.
4. Reduce heat and simmer for 10-15 minutes, until vegetables are tender.
5. Stir in snow peas and lime juice. Cook for another 2 minutes.
6. Season with salt and pepper. Serve hot.

27. THAI COCONUT SOUP

Ingredients:

- 2 tbsp coconut oil

- 1 large onion, chopped
- 3 cloves garlic, minced
- 1 tbsp fresh ginger, minced
- 2 cups mushrooms, sliced
- 4 cups low-sodium vegetable broth
- 1 can (15 oz) coconut milk
- 2 tbsp fish sauce (optional)
- 1 tbsp lime juice
- 1 cup baby corn, chopped
- 1 cup cherry tomatoes, halved
- Fresh cilantro, chopped
- Salt and pepper to taste

Instructions:

1. Heat coconut oil in a large pot over medium heat. Add onion and cook until softened, about 5 minutes.
2. Add garlic and ginger, and cook for another minute.
3. Stir in mushrooms and cook until tender, about 5 minutes.
4. Add broth, coconut milk, fish sauce, and lime juice. Bring to a boil.
5. Reduce heat and simmer for 10 minutes.
6. Add baby corn and cherry tomatoes. Cook for another 5 minutes.
7. Season with salt and pepper. Garnish with fresh cilantro. Serve hot.

28. LEMON CHICKEN SOUP

Ingredients:

- 2 tbsp olive oil
- 1 large onion, chopped
- 3 cloves garlic, minced
- 2 boneless, skinless chicken breasts, cubed
- 6 cups low-sodium chicken broth
- 1 cup carrots, sliced
- 1 cup celery, sliced

- 1/2 cup quinoa, rinsed
- Juice of 2 lemons
- Fresh parsley, chopped
- Salt and pepper to taste

Instructions:

1. Heat olive oil in a large pot over medium heat. Add onion and cook until softened, about 5 minutes.
2. Add garlic and chicken, and cook until chicken is browned, about 5 minutes.
3. Stir in broth, carrots, celery, and quinoa. Bring to a boil.
4. Reduce heat and simmer for 20-25 minutes, until quinoa is tender and chicken is cooked through.
5. Stir in lemon juice and parsley. Season with salt and pepper.
6. Serve hot.

29. CUCUMBER DILL SOUP

Ingredients:

- 2 tbsp olive oil
- 1 large onion, chopped
- 3 cloves garlic, minced
- 4 large cucumbers, peeled, seeded, and chopped
- 4 cups low-sodium vegetable broth
- 1 cup low-fat yogurt or almond yogurt
- 2 tbsp fresh dill, chopped
- Juice of 1 lemon
- Salt and pepper to taste

Instructions:

1. Heat olive oil in a large pot over medium heat. Add onion and cook until softened, about 5 minutes.
2. Add garlic and cook for another minute.
3. Stir in cucumbers and broth. Bring to a boil.

4. Reduce heat and simmer for 15-20 minutes, until cucumbers are tender.
5. Use an immersion blender to puree the soup until smooth.
6. Stir in yogurt, dill, and lemon juice. Heat through without boiling.
7. Season with salt and pepper. Serve chilled or hot.

30. BEETROOT SOUP

Ingredients:

- 2 tbsp olive oil
- 1 large onion, chopped
- 3 cloves garlic, minced
- 4 large beets, peeled and chopped
- 4 cups low-sodium vegetable broth
- 1 cup orange juice
- 1 tbsp fresh ginger, minced
- Salt and pepper to taste
- Sour cream or yogurt for garnish

Instructions:

1. Heat olive oil in a large pot over medium heat. Add onion and cook until softened, about 5 minutes.
2. Add garlic and ginger, and cook for another minute.
3. Stir in beets, broth, and orange juice. Bring to a boil.
4. Reduce heat and simmer for 30-35 minutes, until beets are tender.
5. Use an immersion blender to puree the soup until smooth.
6. Season with salt and pepper. Serve hot with a dollop of sour cream or yogurt.

31. SWEET CORN SOUP

Ingredients:

- 2 tbsp olive oil
- 1 large onion, chopped
- 3 cloves garlic, minced
- 4 cups corn kernels (fresh or frozen)
- 4 cups low-sodium vegetable broth
- 1 cup low-fat milk or almond milk
- 1 tsp smoked paprika
- Salt and pepper to taste

Instructions:

1. Heat olive oil in a large pot over medium heat. Add onion and cook until softened, about 5 minutes.
2. Add garlic and smoked paprika, and cook for another minute.
3. Stir in corn and broth. Bring to a boil.
4. Reduce heat and simmer for 15-20 minutes.
5. Use an immersion blender to puree the soup to your desired consistency.
6. Stir in milk. Heat through without boiling.
7. Season with salt and pepper. Serve hot.

32. CURRIED PUMPKIN SOUP

Ingredients:

- 2 tbsp olive oil
- 1 large onion, chopped
- 3 cloves garlic, minced
- 1 tbsp fresh ginger, minced
- 4 cups pumpkin puree (canned or fresh)
- 4 cups low-sodium vegetable broth
- 1 can (15 oz) coconut milk
- 1 tbsp curry powder
- Salt and pepper to taste

Instructions:

1. Heat olive oil in a large pot over medium heat. Add onion and cook until softened, about 5 minutes.
2. Add garlic, ginger, and curry powder, and cook for another minute.
3. Stir in pumpkin puree and broth. Bring to a boil.
4. Reduce heat and simmer for 15 minutes.
5. Stir in coconut milk. Heat through without boiling.
6. Season with salt and pepper. Serve hot.

33. DETOX VEGETABLE SOUP

Ingredients:

- 2 tbsp olive oil
- 1 large onion, chopped
- 3 cloves garlic, minced
- 3 carrots, chopped
- 2 celery stalks, chopped
- 1 zucchini, chopped
- 1 cup broccoli florets
- 6 cups low-sodium vegetable broth
- 1 can (15 oz) diced tomatoes (no salt added)
- 1 tsp dried thyme
- 1 tsp dried oregano
- 2 cups fresh spinach, chopped
- Salt and pepper to taste

Instructions:

1. Heat olive oil in a large pot over medium heat. Add onion, carrots, and celery. Cook until softened, about 5-7 minutes.
2. Add garlic and cook for another minute.
3. Stir in zucchini, broccoli, broth, tomatoes, thyme, and oregano. Bring to a boil.
4. Reduce heat and simmer for 20-25 minutes, until vegetables are tender.
5. Stir in spinach and cook until wilted, about 2 minutes.
6. Season with salt and pepper. Serve hot.

34. GARLIC SOUP

Ingredients:

- 2 tbsp olive oil
- 2 large heads of garlic, cloves peeled and sliced
- 1 large onion, chopped
- 4 cups low-sodium vegetable broth
- 1 cup low-fat milk or almond milk
- 1 tsp dried thyme
- Salt and pepper to taste
- Fresh parsley, chopped, for garnish

Instructions:

1. Heat olive oil in a large pot over medium heat. Add onion and garlic. Cook until softened, about 5-7 minutes.
2. Stir in broth and thyme. Bring to a boil.
3. Reduce heat and simmer for 20-25 minutes.
4. Use an immersion blender to puree the soup until smooth.
5. Stir in milk. Heat through without boiling.
6. Season with salt and pepper. Garnish with fresh parsley. Serve hot.

35. CHICKEN AND RICE SOUP

Ingredients:

- 2 tbsp olive oil
- 1 large onion, chopped
- 3 cloves garlic, minced
- 2 boneless, skinless chicken breasts, cubed
- 6 cups low-sodium chicken broth
- 1 cup carrots, sliced
- 1 cup celery, sliced
- 1 cup brown rice
- 1 tsp dried thyme

- Salt and pepper to taste
- Fresh parsley, chopped, for garnish

Instructions:

1. Heat olive oil in a large pot over medium heat. Add onion and cook until softened, about 5 minutes.
2. Add garlic and chicken, and cook until chicken is browned, about 5 minutes.
3. Stir in broth, carrots, celery, rice, and thyme. Bring to a boil.
4. Reduce heat and simmer for 30-35 minutes, until rice is tender and chicken is cooked through.
5. Season with salt and pepper. Garnish with fresh parsley. Serve hot.

36. CREAMY TOMATO SOUP

Ingredients:

- 2 tbsp olive oil
- 1 large onion, chopped
- 3 cloves garlic, minced
- 2 cans (15 oz each) diced tomatoes (no salt added)
- 4 cups low-sodium vegetable broth
- 1 cup low-fat milk or almond milk
- 1 tsp dried basil
- Salt and pepper to taste

Instructions:

1. Heat olive oil in a large pot over medium heat. Add onion and cook until softened, about 5 minutes.
2. Add garlic and cook for another minute.
3. Stir in tomatoes, broth, and basil. Bring to a boil.
4. Reduce heat and simmer for 15-20 minutes.
5. Use an immersion blender to puree the soup until smooth.
6. Stir in milk. Heat through without boiling.
7. Season with salt and pepper. Serve hot.

37. MUSHROOM AND WILD RICE SOUP

Ingredients:

- 2 tbsp olive oil
- 1 large onion, chopped
- 3 cloves garlic, minced
- 4 cups mushrooms, sliced
- 1 cup wild rice, rinsed
- 6 cups low-sodium vegetable broth
- 1 tsp dried thyme
- 1 cup low-fat milk or almond milk
- Salt and pepper to taste

Instructions:

1. Heat olive oil in a large pot over medium heat. Add onion and cook until softened, about 5 minutes.
2. Add garlic and mushrooms, and cook until mushrooms are tender, about 5-7 minutes.
3. Stir in wild rice, broth, and thyme. Bring to a boil.
4. Reduce heat and simmer for 45-50 minutes, until rice is tender.
5. Stir in milk. Heat through without boiling.
6. Season with salt and pepper. Serve hot.

38. BLACK BEAN SOUP

Ingredients:

- 2 tbsp olive oil
- 1 large onion, chopped
- 3 cloves garlic, minced
- 1 bell pepper, chopped
- 2 cans (15 oz each) black beans, drained and rinsed
- 4 cups low-sodium vegetable broth
- 1 tsp cumin

- 1 tsp smoked paprika
- 1 can (15 oz) diced tomatoes (no salt added)
- Salt and pepper to taste
- Fresh cilantro, chopped, for garnish

Instructions:

1. Heat olive oil in a large pot over medium heat. Add onion and bell pepper. Cook until softened, about 5-7 minutes.
2. Add garlic, cumin, and smoked paprika, and cook for another minute.
3. Stir in black beans, tomatoes, and broth. Bring to a boil.
4. Reduce heat and simmer for 20-25 minutes.
5. Use an immersion blender to puree the soup to your desired consistency.
6. Season with salt and pepper. Garnish with fresh cilantro. Serve hot.

39. WHITE BEAN AND KALE SOUP

Ingredients:

- 2 tbsp olive oil
- 1 large onion, chopped
- 3 cloves garlic, minced
- 2 cans (15 oz each) white beans, drained and rinsed
- 6 cups low-sodium vegetable broth
- 1 bunch kale, chopped
- 1 tsp dried thyme
- 1 tsp dried rosemary
- Salt and pepper to taste

Instructions:

1. Heat olive oil in a large pot over medium heat. Add onion and cook until softened, about 5 minutes.
2. Add garlic, thyme, and rosemary, and cook for another minute.

3. Stir in white beans and broth. Bring to a boil.
4. Reduce heat and simmer for 15-20 minutes.
5. Add kale and cook until wilted, about 5 minutes.
6. Season with salt and pepper. Serve hot.

40. TURMERIC GINGER SOUP

Ingredients:

- 2 tbsp olive oil
- 1 large onion, chopped
- 3 cloves garlic, minced
- 1 tbsp fresh ginger, minced
- 1 tsp ground turmeric
- 4 large carrots, peeled and chopped
- 4 cups low-sodium vegetable broth
- 1 cup low-fat milk or almond milk
- Salt and pepper to taste

Instructions:

1. Heat olive oil in a large pot over medium heat. Add onion and cook until softened, about 5 minutes.
2. Add garlic, ginger, and turmeric, and cook for another minute.
3. Stir in carrots and broth. Bring to a boil.
4. Reduce heat and simmer for 20-25 minutes, until carrots are tender.
5. Use an immersion blender to puree the soup until smooth.
6. Stir in milk. Heat through without boiling.
7. Season with salt and pepper. Serve hot.

41. BROCCOLI POTATO SOUP

Ingredients:

- 2 tbsp olive oil

- 1 large onion, chopped
- 3 cloves garlic, minced
- 4 cups broccoli florets
- 4 cups potatoes, peeled and diced
- 6 cups low-sodium vegetable broth
- 1 cup low-fat milk or almond milk
- Salt and pepper to taste

Instructions:

1. Heat olive oil in a large pot over medium heat. Add onion and cook until softened, about 5 minutes.
2. Add garlic and cook for another minute.
3. Stir in broccoli, potatoes, and broth. Bring to a boil.
4. Reduce heat and simmer for 20-25 minutes, until vegetables are tender.
5. Use an immersion blender to puree the soup until smooth.
6. Stir in milk. Heat through without boiling.
7. Season with salt and pepper. Serve hot.

42. SUMMER SQUASH SOUP

Ingredients:

- 2 tbsp olive oil
- 1 large onion, chopped
- 3 cloves garlic, minced
- 4 cups summer squash, chopped
- 4 cups low-sodium vegetable broth
- 1 tsp dried thyme
- Salt and pepper to taste

Instructions:

1. Heat olive oil in a large pot over medium heat. Add onion and cook until softened, about 5 minutes.
2. Add garlic and cook for another minute.
3. Stir in squash, broth, and thyme. Bring to a boil.

4. Reduce heat and simmer for 15-20 minutes, until squash is tender.
5. Use an immersion blender to puree the soup until smooth.
6. Season with salt and pepper. Serve hot.

43. FRENCH ONION SOUP

Ingredients:

- 2 tbsp olive oil
- 6 large onions, thinly sliced
- 3 cloves garlic, minced
- 8 cups low-sodium beef broth
- 1 cup dry white wine
- 1 tsp dried thyme
- Salt and pepper to taste
- Whole grain bread, sliced and toasted
- 1 cup low-fat shredded Gruyère cheese

Instructions:

1. Heat olive oil in a large pot over medium heat. Add onions and cook, stirring frequently, until caramelized, about 25-30 minutes.
2. Add garlic and cook for another minute.
3. Stir in broth, wine, and thyme. Bring to a boil.
4. Reduce heat and simmer for 30 minutes.
5. Season with salt and pepper.
6. Ladle soup into oven-safe bowls, top with a slice of toasted bread, and sprinkle with cheese.
7. Broil until cheese is melted and bubbly. Serve hot.

44. PEA AND HAM SOUP

Ingredients:

- 2 tbsp olive oil

- 1 large onion, chopped
- 3 cloves garlic, minced
- 4 cups split peas, rinsed
- 8 cups low-sodium vegetable broth
- 1 cup diced ham
- 2 carrots, chopped
- 2 celery stalks, chopped
- 1 bay leaf
- Salt and pepper to taste

Instructions:

1. Heat olive oil in a large pot over medium heat. Add onion and cook until softened, about 5 minutes.
2. Add garlic and cook for another minute.
3. Stir in split peas, broth, ham, carrots, celery, and bay leaf. Bring to a boil.
4. Reduce heat and simmer for 45-50 minutes, until peas are tender.
5. Remove bay leaf.
6. Season with salt and pepper. Serve hot.

45. CHILLED AVOCADO SOUP

Ingredients:

- 4 ripe avocados, peeled and pitted
- 4 cups low-sodium vegetable broth, chilled
- 1 cup low-fat yogurt
- 1 cucumber, peeled and chopped
- 2 tbsp lime juice
- 2 tbsp fresh cilantro, chopped
- Salt and pepper to taste

Instructions:

1. In a blender, combine avocados, broth, yogurt, cucumber, lime juice, and cilantro.

2. Blend until smooth.
3. Season with salt and pepper.
4. Chill in the refrigerator for at least 1 hour before serving. Serve cold.

46. LENTIL AND SPINACH SOUP

Ingredients:

- 2 tbsp olive oil
- 1 large onion, chopped
- 3 cloves garlic, minced
- 1 cup lentils, rinsed
- 6 cups low-sodium vegetable broth
- 2 carrots, chopped
- 2 celery stalks, chopped
- 1 tsp dried thyme
- 1 tsp cumin
- 4 cups fresh spinach, chopped
- Salt and pepper to taste

Instructions:

1. Heat olive oil in a large pot over medium heat. Add onion and cook until softened, about 5 minutes.
2. Add garlic and cook for another minute.
3. Stir in lentils, broth, carrots, celery, thyme, and cumin. Bring to a boil.
4. Reduce heat and simmer for 30-35 minutes, until lentils are tender.
5. Stir in spinach and cook until wilted, about 2 minutes.
6. Season with salt and pepper. Serve hot.

47. RED LENTIL SOUP

Ingredients:

- 2 tbsp olive oil
- 1 large onion, chopped
- 3 cloves garlic, minced
- 1 cup red lentils, rinsed
- 6 cups low-sodium vegetable broth
- 2 carrots, chopped
- 2 celery stalks, chopped
- 1 tsp ground cumin
- 1 tsp ground coriander
- Salt and pepper to taste

Instructions:

1. Heat olive oil in a large pot over medium heat. Add onion and cook until softened, about 5 minutes.
2. Add garlic, cumin, and coriander, and cook for another minute.
3. Stir in lentils, broth, carrots, and celery. Bring to a boil.
4. Reduce heat and simmer for 20-25 minutes, until lentils are tender.
5. Season with salt and pepper. Serve hot.

48. MOROCCAN CHICKPEA SOUP

Ingredients:

- 2 tbsp olive oil
- 1 large onion, chopped
- 3 cloves garlic, minced
- 2 cans (15 oz each) chickpeas, drained and rinsed
- 6 cups low-sodium vegetable broth
- 1 can (15 oz) diced tomatoes (no salt added)
- 1 tsp ground cumin
- 1 tsp ground cinnamon
- 1 tsp ground coriander
- 1 tsp ground turmeric
- Salt and pepper to taste
- Fresh cilantro, chopped, for garnish

Instructions:

1. Heat olive oil in a large pot over medium heat. Add onion and cook until softened, about 5 minutes.
2. Add garlic, cumin, cinnamon, coriander, and turmeric, and cook for another minute.
3. Stir in chickpeas, tomatoes, and broth. Bring to a boil.
4. Reduce heat and simmer for 20-25 minutes.
5. Season with salt and pepper. Garnish with fresh cilantro. Serve hot.

49. ARTICHOKE SOUP

Ingredients:

- 2 tbsp olive oil
- 1 large onion, chopped
- 3 cloves garlic, minced
- 4 cups artichoke hearts (fresh or canned, drained)
- 6 cups low-sodium vegetable broth
- 1 cup low-fat milk or almond milk
- 1 tsp dried thyme
- Salt and pepper to taste

Instructions:

1. Heat olive oil in a large pot over medium heat. Add onion and cook until softened, about 5 minutes.
2. Add garlic and cook for another minute.
3. Stir in artichokes, broth, and thyme. Bring to a boil.
4. Reduce heat and simmer for 20-25 minutes, until artichokes are tender.
5. Use an immersion blender to puree the soup until smooth.
6. Stir in milk. Heat through without boiling.
7. Season with salt and pepper. Serve hot.

50. LEMON LENTIL SOUP

Ingredients:

- 2 tbsp olive oil
- 1 large onion, chopped
- 3 cloves garlic, minced
- 1 cup lentils, rinsed
- 6 cups low-sodium vegetable broth
- 2 carrots, chopped
- 2 celery stalks, chopped
- 1 tsp dried thyme
- Juice of 1 lemon
- Salt and pepper to taste
- Fresh parsley, chopped, for garnish

Instructions:

1. Heat olive oil in a large pot over medium heat. Add onion and cook until softened, about 5 minutes.
2. Add garlic and cook for another minute.
3. Stir in lentils, broth, carrots, celery, and thyme. Bring to a boil.
4. Reduce heat and simmer for 30-35 minutes, until lentils are tender.
5. Stir in lemon juice.
6. Season with salt and pepper. Garnish with fresh parsley. Serve hot.

51. BELL PEPPER SOUP

Ingredients:

- 2 tbsp olive oil
- 1 large onion, chopped
- 3 cloves garlic, minced
- 4 bell peppers, any color, chopped
- 4 cups low-sodium vegetable broth
- 1 tsp smoked paprika
- 1 cup low-fat milk or almond milk

- Salt and pepper to taste

Instructions:

1. Heat olive oil in a large pot over medium heat. Add onion and cook until softened, about 5 minutes.
2. Add garlic and smoked paprika, and cook for another minute.
3. Stir in bell peppers and broth. Bring to a boil.
4. Reduce heat and simmer for 15-20 minutes, until peppers are tender.
5. Use an immersion blender to puree the soup until smooth.
6. Stir in milk. Heat through without boiling.
7. Season with salt and pepper. Serve hot.

52. CAULIFLOWER SOUP

Ingredients:

- 2 tbsp olive oil
- 1 large onion, chopped
- 3 cloves garlic, minced
- 1 head cauliflower, chopped
- 4 cups low-sodium vegetable broth
- 1 cup low-fat milk or almond milk
- Salt and pepper to taste
- Fresh chives, chopped, for garnish

Instructions:

1. Heat olive oil in a large pot over medium heat. Add onion and cook until softened, about 5 minutes.
2. Add garlic and cook for another minute.
3. Stir in cauliflower and broth. Bring to a boil.
4. Reduce heat and simmer for 15-20 minutes, until cauliflower is tender.
5. Use an immersion blender to puree the soup until smooth.
6. Stir in milk. Heat through without boiling.

7. Season with salt and pepper. Garnish with fresh chives. Serve hot.

53. DILL PICKLE SOUP

Ingredients:

- 2 tbsp unsalted butter
- 1 large onion, chopped
- 3 cloves garlic, minced
- 4 cups low-sodium vegetable broth
- 4 large dill pickles, chopped
- 1/2 cup pickle juice
- 2 large potatoes, peeled and diced
- 1 cup low-fat sour cream
- Salt and pepper to taste
- Fresh dill, chopped, for garnish

Instructions:

1. In a large pot, melt the butter over medium heat. Add onion and cook until softened, about 5 minutes.
2. Add garlic and cook for another minute.
3. Stir in broth, pickles, pickle juice, and potatoes. Bring to a boil.
4. Reduce heat and simmer for 20-25 minutes, until potatoes are tender.
5. Remove from heat and stir in sour cream.
6. Use an immersion blender to puree the soup until smooth.
7. Season with salt and pepper. Garnish with fresh dill. Serve hot.

54. ROOT VEGETABLE SOUP

Ingredients:

- 2 tbsp olive oil

- 1 large onion, chopped
- 3 cloves garlic, minced
- 2 carrots, peeled and chopped
- 2 parsnips, peeled and chopped
- 2 turnips, peeled and chopped
- 1 sweet potato, peeled and chopped
- 6 cups low-sodium vegetable broth
- 1 tsp dried thyme
- Salt and pepper to taste
- Fresh parsley, chopped, for garnish

Instructions:

1. Heat olive oil in a large pot over medium heat. Add onion and cook until softened, about 5 minutes.
2. Add garlic and cook for another minute.
3. Stir in carrots, parsnips, turnips, sweet potato, broth, and thyme. Bring to a boil.
4. Reduce heat and simmer for 20-25 minutes, until vegetables are tender.
5. Use an immersion blender to puree the soup until smooth.
6. Season with salt and pepper. Garnish with fresh parsley. Serve hot.

55. PEANUT BUTTER SOUP

Ingredients:

- 2 tbsp olive oil
- 1 large onion, chopped
- 3 cloves garlic, minced
- 1 red bell pepper, chopped
- 1 sweet potato, peeled and diced
- 1 can (15 oz) diced tomatoes (no salt added)
- 1/2 cup peanut butter
- 4 cups low-sodium vegetable broth
- 1/2 cup coconut milk
- 1 tsp ground cumin

- 1 tsp paprika
- Salt and pepper to taste
- Fresh cilantro, chopped, for garnish

Instructions:

1. Heat olive oil in a large pot over medium heat. Add onion and cook until softened, about 5 minutes.
2. Add garlic and cook for another minute.
3. Stir in bell pepper, sweet potato, and tomatoes. Cook for 5 minutes, stirring occasionally.
4. Add peanut butter, broth, coconut milk, cumin, and paprika. Stir until well combined.
5. Bring to a simmer and cook for 20-25 minutes, until sweet potatoes are tender.
6. Use an immersion blender to puree the soup until smooth.
7. Season with salt and pepper. Garnish with fresh cilantro. Serve hot.

56. ITALIAN WEDDING SOUP

Ingredients:

- 1 tbsp olive oil
- 1 large onion, chopped
- 3 cloves garlic, minced
- 2 carrots, chopped
- 2 celery stalks, chopped
- 6 cups low-sodium chicken broth
- 1 cup small pasta (such as orzo or acini di pepe)
- 1 bunch spinach, chopped
- 1 lb lean ground turkey or chicken
- 1/4 cup breadcrumbs
- 1/4 cup grated Parmesan cheese
- 1 egg
- 1 tsp dried oregano
- Salt and pepper to taste
- Fresh parsley, chopped, for garnish

Instructions:

1. In a bowl, mix together ground turkey, breadcrumbs, Parmesan cheese, egg, oregano, salt, and pepper. Form into small meatballs.
2. In a large pot, heat olive oil over medium heat. Add onion, garlic, carrots, and celery. Cook until softened, about 5-7 minutes.
3. Add chicken broth to the pot and bring to a simmer.
4. Drop meatballs into the broth and simmer for 10 minutes.
5. Stir in pasta and cook according to package instructions.
6. Stir in spinach and cook until wilted, about 2 minutes.
7. Season with salt and pepper. Garnish with fresh parsley. Serve hot.

57. SPINACH AND TOFU SOUP

Ingredients:

- 1 tbsp olive oil
- 1 large onion, chopped
- 3 cloves garlic, minced
- 1 block (14 oz) firm tofu, drained and cubed
- 6 cups low-sodium vegetable broth
- 4 cups fresh spinach
- 2 tbsp soy sauce
- 1 tsp sesame oil
- Salt and pepper to taste
- Green onions, chopped, for garnish

Instructions:

1. Heat olive oil in a large pot over medium heat. Add onion and cook until softened, about 5 minutes.
2. Add garlic and cook for another minute.
3. Stir in tofu and vegetable broth. Bring to a simmer.
4. Cook for 10 minutes.

5. Stir in spinach, soy sauce, and sesame oil. Cook until spinach wilts, about 2-3 minutes.
6. Season with salt and pepper.
7. Garnish with green onions before serving. Serve hot.

58. DETOX GREEN SOUP

Ingredients:

- 1 tbsp olive oil
- 1 large onion, chopped
- 2 cloves garlic, minced
- 4 cups low-sodium vegetable broth
- 4 cups spinach
- 2 cups kale, chopped
- 1 zucchini, chopped
- 1 cup broccoli florets
- 1 cup green peas
- Juice of 1 lemon
- Salt and pepper to taste

Instructions:

1. Heat olive oil in a large pot over medium heat. Add onion and cook until softened, about 5 minutes.
2. Add garlic and cook for another minute.
3. Stir in vegetable broth, spinach, kale, zucchini, broccoli, and peas. Bring to a boil.
4. Reduce heat and simmer for 15-20 minutes, until vegetables are tender.
5. Remove from heat and let cool slightly.
6. Blend the soup until smooth using a blender or immersion blender.
7. Stir in lemon juice. Season with salt and pepper.
8. Serve hot or warm.

59. COCONUT LIME SOUP

Ingredients:

- 1 tbsp coconut oil
- 1 onion, chopped
- 2 cloves garlic, minced
- 1 red bell pepper, chopped
- 1 green bell pepper, chopped
- 1 can (14 oz) coconut milk
- 4 cups vegetable broth
- 2 tbsp soy sauce
- Juice of 2 limes
- Zest of 1 lime
- 1 tsp red curry paste (optional)
- Salt and pepper to taste
- Fresh cilantro, chopped, for garnish

Instructions:

1. Heat coconut oil in a large pot over medium heat. Add onion and garlic, sauté until softened, about 5 minutes.
2. Add red and green bell peppers, cook for another 3-4 minutes.
3. Pour in coconut milk and vegetable broth, bring to a simmer.
4. Stir in soy sauce, lime juice, lime zest, and red curry paste (if using). Simmer for 10-15 minutes.
5. Season with salt and pepper.
6. Serve hot, garnished with fresh cilantro.

60. APPLE BUTTERNUT SQUASH SOUP

Ingredients:

- 1 tbsp olive oil
- 1 onion, chopped
- 3 cloves garlic, minced
- 1 butternut squash, peeled, seeded, and chopped
- 2 apples, peeled, cored, and chopped
- 4 cups vegetable broth

- 1 tsp ground cinnamon
- 1/2 tsp ground nutmeg
- Salt and pepper to taste
- 1/2 cup coconut milk (optional)
- Toasted pumpkin seeds, for garnish

Instructions:

1. Heat olive oil in a large pot over medium heat. Add onion and garlic, cook until softened, about 5 minutes.
2. Add butternut squash and apples, cook for another 5 minutes.
3. Pour in vegetable broth, add cinnamon and nutmeg. Bring to a boil, then reduce heat and simmer for 20-25 minutes, or until squash and apples are tender.
4. Use an immersion blender to puree the soup until smooth.
5. Stir in coconut milk (if using). Season with salt and pepper.
6. Serve hot, garnished with toasted pumpkin seeds.

61. GREEN GODDESS SOUP

Ingredients:

- 1 tbsp olive oil
- 1 onion, chopped
- 2 cloves garlic, minced
- 1 head broccoli, chopped
- 1 head cauliflower, chopped
- 4 cups vegetable broth
- 1 cup spinach leaves
- 1 avocado, peeled and pitted
- Juice of 1 lemon
- Salt and pepper to taste
- Fresh parsley, chopped, for garnish

Instructions:

1. Heat olive oil in a large pot over medium heat. Add onion and garlic, sauté until softened, about 5 minutes.
2. Add broccoli, cauliflower, and vegetable broth. Bring to a boil, then reduce heat and simmer for 15-20 minutes, or until vegetables are tender.
3. Stir in spinach leaves and cook for an additional 2-3 minutes until wilted.
4. Remove from heat and let cool slightly.
5. Transfer the soup to a blender. Add avocado and lemon juice. Blend until smooth.
6. Season with salt and pepper to taste.
7. Serve hot, garnished with fresh parsley.

62. VEGETABLE NOODLE SOUP

Ingredients:

- 1 tbsp olive oil
- 1 onion, chopped
- 2 cloves garlic, minced
- 2 carrots, sliced
- 2 celery stalks, sliced
- 6 cups vegetable broth
- 2 cups cooked noodles of your choice
- 1 cup green beans, chopped
- 1 cup corn kernels
- Salt and pepper to taste
- Fresh parsley, chopped, for garnish

Instructions:

1. Heat olive oil in a large pot over medium heat. Add onion and garlic, sauté until softened, about 5 minutes.
2. Add carrots, celery, and vegetable broth. Bring to a boil, then reduce heat and simmer for 10 minutes.
3. Stir in cooked noodles, green beans, and corn kernels. Simmer for an additional 5-7 minutes, or until vegetables are tender.

4. Season with salt and pepper to taste.
5. Serve hot, garnished with fresh parsley.

63. LEEK AND POTATO SOUP

Ingredients:

- 2 tbsp butter
- 2 leeks, sliced
- 3 potatoes, peeled and diced
- 4 cups vegetable broth
- 1 cup milk or heavy cream
- Salt and pepper to taste
- Fresh chives, chopped, for garnish

Instructions:

1. In a large pot, melt the butter over medium heat. Add the leeks and cook until softened, about 5 minutes.
2. Add the diced potatoes and vegetable broth. Bring to a boil, then reduce heat and simmer for 15-20 minutes, or until the potatoes are tender.
3. Use an immersion blender to puree the soup until smooth.
4. Stir in the milk or cream. Heat through but do not boil.
5. Season with salt and pepper.
6. Garnish with fresh chives before serving. Serve hot.

64. SESAME MISO SOUP

Ingredients:

- 4 cups vegetable broth
- 3 tbsp miso paste
- 1 tbsp soy sauce
- 1 tsp sesame oil
- 1 block (14 oz) firm tofu, diced
- 2 green onions, chopped

- 1/4 cup seaweed (such as wakame or nori), chopped

Instructions:

1. In a large pot, bring vegetable broth to a simmer over medium heat.
2. In a small bowl, whisk together miso paste and soy sauce until well combined. Stir the mixture into the simmering broth.
3. Add sesame oil, tofu, green onions, and seaweed to the pot.
4. Simmer for 5-7 minutes, stirring occasionally, until the tofu is heated through and the seaweed is softened.
5. Taste and adjust seasoning if needed.
6. Serve hot.

65. SEAWEED AND TOFU SOUP

Ingredients:

- 4 cups vegetable broth
- 1 block (14 oz) firm tofu, diced
- 1/4 cup dried seaweed (such as wakame)
- 2 green onions, chopped
- 2 tbsp soy sauce
- 1 tbsp rice vinegar
- 1 tsp sesame oil
- Salt and pepper to taste

Instructions:

1. In a large pot, bring vegetable broth to a simmer over medium heat.
2. Add tofu and dried seaweed to the pot. Simmer for 5 minutes.
3. Stir in green onions, soy sauce, rice vinegar, and sesame oil.
4. Simmer for another 2-3 minutes.
5. Season with salt and pepper to taste.
6. Serve hot.

66. CREAMY CAULIFLOWER SOUP

Ingredients:

- 1 head cauliflower, chopped
- 2 cloves garlic, minced
- 1 onion, chopped
- 4 cups vegetable broth
- 1 cup milk or heavy cream
- 2 tbsp olive oil
- Salt and pepper to taste
- Fresh chives, chopped, for garnish

Instructions:

1. Heat olive oil in a large pot over medium heat. Add garlic and onion, sauté until softened, about 5 minutes.
2. Add cauliflower and vegetable broth to the pot. Bring to a boil, then reduce heat and simmer for 15-20 minutes, or until cauliflower is tender.
3. Use an immersion blender to puree the soup until smooth.
4. Stir in milk or heavy cream. Heat through but do not boil.
5. Season with salt and pepper to taste.
6. Garnish with fresh chives before serving. Serve hot.

67. CHICKPEA VEGETABLE SOUP

Ingredients:

- 1 tbsp olive oil
- 1 onion, chopped
- 2 carrots, diced
- 2 celery stalks, diced
- 3 cloves garlic, minced
- 1 can (15 oz) chickpeas, drained and rinsed
- 1 can (14 oz) diced tomatoes
- 4 cups vegetable broth

- 1 tsp dried thyme
- 1 tsp dried oregano
- Salt and pepper to taste
- Fresh parsley, chopped, for garnish

Instructions:

1. Heat olive oil in a large pot over medium heat. Add onion, carrots, and celery. Cook until vegetables are softened, about 5-7 minutes.
2. Add garlic and cook for another minute.
3. Stir in chickpeas, diced tomatoes, vegetable broth, thyme, and oregano. Bring to a boil.
4. Reduce heat and simmer for 15-20 minutes.
5. Season with salt and pepper to taste.
6. Garnish with fresh parsley before serving. Serve hot.

68. GREEN LENTIL SOUP

Ingredients:

- 1 cup green lentils, rinsed
- 4 cups vegetable broth
- 1 onion, chopped
- 2 carrots, chopped
- 2 celery stalks, chopped
- 2 cloves garlic, minced
- 1 tsp ground cumin
- 1 tsp ground coriander
- Salt and pepper to taste
- Fresh cilantro, chopped, for garnish

Instructions:

1. In a large pot, combine vegetable broth, lentils, onion, carrots, celery, garlic, cumin, and coriander.
2. Bring to a boil over medium-high heat.

3. Reduce heat to low, cover, and simmer for 25-30 minutes, or until lentils and vegetables are tender.
4. Season with salt and pepper to taste.
5. Garnish with fresh cilantro before serving. Serve hot.

69. TOMATO RICE SOUP

Ingredients:

- 1 tbsp olive oil
- 1 onion, chopped
- 2 carrots, diced
- 2 celery stalks, diced
- 2 cloves garlic, minced
- 1 can (14 oz) diced tomatoes
- 1/2 cup white rice
- 4 cups vegetable broth
- 1 tsp dried thyme
- Salt and pepper to taste
- Fresh basil, chopped, for garnish

Instructions:

1. Heat olive oil in a large pot over medium heat. Add onion, carrots, and celery. Cook until vegetables are softened, about 5-7 minutes.
2. Add garlic and cook for another minute.
3. Stir in diced tomatoes, rice, vegetable broth, and thyme. Bring to a boil.
4. Reduce heat and simmer for 20-25 minutes, or until rice is cooked and vegetables are tender.
5. Season with salt and pepper to taste.
6. Garnish with fresh basil before serving. Serve hot.

70. CREAM OF MUSHROOM SOUP

Ingredients:

- 2 tbsp unsalted butter
- 1 onion, chopped
- 2 cloves garlic, minced
- 1 lb mushrooms, sliced
- 4 cups vegetable broth
- 1 cup heavy cream
- 2 tbsp all-purpose flour
- Salt and pepper to taste
- Fresh parsley, chopped, for garnish

Instructions:

1. In a large pot, melt the butter over medium heat. Add onion and cook until softened, about 5 minutes.
2. Add garlic and cook for another minute.
3. Stir in mushrooms and cook until they release their juices and become golden brown, about 8-10 minutes.
4. Sprinkle flour over the mushrooms and stir to coat.
5. Gradually pour in vegetable broth while stirring constantly to prevent lumps from forming.
6. Bring the soup to a simmer and cook for 10-15 minutes, or until slightly thickened.
7. Stir in heavy cream and simmer for another 5 minutes.
8. Season with salt and pepper to taste.
9. Garnish with fresh chopped parsley before serving. Serve hot

71. PESTO CHICKEN SOUP

Ingredients:

- 1 lb chicken breast, cooked and shredded
- 4 cups chicken broth
- 1 cup pesto sauce
- 2 cups spinach leaves
- 1 cup diced tomatoes
- 1 cup diced carrots
- 1 cup diced celery
- 1 cup diced onion

- 1/2 cup orzo pasta
- Salt and pepper to taste

Instructions:

1. In a large pot, sauté the onion, carrots, and celery until softened.
2. Add the chicken broth and bring to a boil.
3. Stir in the orzo pasta and cook until tender, about 10 minutes.
4. Add the shredded chicken, diced tomatoes, and spinach leaves.
5. Stir in the pesto sauce and simmer for an additional 5 minutes.
6. Season with salt and pepper to taste and serve hot.

72. SAUSAGE AND KALE SOUP

Ingredients:

- 1 lb Italian sausage, sliced
- 4 cups chicken broth
- 1 cup chopped kale
- 2 cups diced potatoes
- 1 cup diced carrots
- 1 cup diced celery
- 1 cup diced onion
- 2 cloves garlic, minced
- Salt and pepper to taste

Instructions:

1. In a large pot, cook the sausage until browned. Remove and set aside.
2. In the same pot, sauté the onion, garlic, carrots, and celery until softened.
3. Add the chicken broth and potatoes and bring to a boil.

4. Reduce heat and simmer until potatoes are tender, about 15 minutes.
5. Stir in the cooked sausage and chopped kale.
6. Season with salt and pepper to taste and cook for another 5 minutes before serving.

73. BUTTERNUT APPLE SOUP

Ingredients:

- 1 butternut squash, peeled and cubed
- 2 apples, peeled and chopped
- 4 cups vegetable broth
- 1 cup diced onion
- 2 cloves garlic, minced
- 1 tsp ground cinnamon
- 1/2 tsp ground nutmeg
- 1/2 cup coconut milk
- Salt and pepper to taste

Instructions:

1. In a large pot, sauté the onion and garlic until fragrant.
2. Add the butternut squash, apples, and vegetable broth.
3. Bring to a boil, then reduce heat and simmer until squash and apples are tender, about 20 minutes.
4. Puree the soup with an immersion blender until smooth.
5. Stir in the cinnamon, nutmeg, and coconut milk.
6. Season with salt and pepper to taste and serve hot.

74. HERB CHICKEN SOUP

Ingredients:

- 1 lb chicken breast, cooked and shredded
- 4 cups chicken broth
- 1 cup diced carrots

- 1 cup diced celery
- 1 cup diced onion
- 2 cloves garlic, minced
- 1 tsp dried thyme
- 1 tsp dried rosemary
- 1 bay leaf
- Salt and pepper to taste

Instructions:

1. In a large pot, sauté the onion, garlic, carrots, and celery until softened.
2. Add the chicken broth, thyme, rosemary, and bay leaf.
3. Bring to a boil, then reduce heat and simmer for 15 minutes.
4. Stir in the shredded chicken and cook for an additional 5 minutes.
5. Season with salt and pepper to taste and serve hot.

75. SHRIMP AND CORN SOUP

Ingredients:

- 1 lb shrimp, peeled and deveined
- 4 cups chicken broth
- 2 cups corn kernels (fresh or frozen)
- 1 cup diced potatoes
- 1 cup diced onion
- 1 cup diced celery
- 2 cloves garlic, minced
- 1 cup heavy cream
- 1 tsp paprika
- Salt and pepper to taste

Instructions:

1. In a large pot, sauté the onion, garlic, and celery until softened.
2. Add the chicken broth, potatoes, and corn. Bring to a boil.

3. Reduce heat and simmer until potatoes are tender, about 15 minutes.
4. Stir in the shrimp and cook until they turn pink, about 3 minutes.
5. Add the heavy cream and paprika.
6. Season with salt and pepper to taste and serve hot.

76. CELERIAC SOUP

Ingredients:

- 1 large celeriac (celery root), peeled and diced
- 4 cups vegetable broth
- 1 cup diced onion
- 2 cloves garlic, minced
- 1 cup diced potatoes
- 1/2 cup heavy cream
- Salt and pepper to taste
- Chopped fresh parsley for garnish

Instructions:

1. In a large pot, sauté the onion and garlic until fragrant.
2. Add the celeriac, potatoes, and vegetable broth.
3. Bring to a boil, then reduce heat and simmer until vegetables are tender, about 20 minutes.
4. Puree the soup with an immersion blender until smooth.
5. Stir in the heavy cream.
6. Season with salt and pepper to taste, garnish with parsley, and serve hot.

77. BROCCOLI CASHEW SOUP

Ingredients:

- 1 large head of broccoli, chopped
- 4 cups vegetable broth

- 1 cup raw cashews, soaked for at least 2 hours
- 1 cup diced onion
- 2 cloves garlic, minced
- 1/2 cup nutritional yeast
- Salt and pepper to taste

Instructions:

1. In a large pot, sauté the onion and garlic until fragrant.
2. Add the chopped broccoli and vegetable broth. Bring to a boil.
3. Reduce heat and simmer until broccoli is tender, about 10 minutes.
4. Drain and rinse the cashews, then add to the pot.
5. Puree the soup with an immersion blender until smooth.
6. Stir in the nutritional yeast.
7. Season with salt and pepper to taste and serve hot.

78. DETOX CARROT SOUP

Ingredients:

- 6 large carrots, peeled and chopped
- 4 cups vegetable broth
- 1 cup diced onion
- 2 cloves garlic, minced
- 1 tsp ground turmeric
- 1 tsp ground ginger
- 1/2 cup coconut milk
- Salt and pepper to taste

Instructions:

1. In a large pot, sauté the onion and garlic until fragrant.
2. Add the carrots, turmeric, ginger, and vegetable broth.
3. Bring to a boil, then reduce heat and simmer until carrots are tender, about 20 minutes.
4. Puree the soup with an immersion blender until smooth.

5. Stir in the coconut milk.
6. Season with salt and pepper to taste and serve hot.

79. PEAR AND PARSNIP SOUP

Ingredients:

- 4 large parsnips, peeled and chopped
- 2 pears, peeled and chopped
- 4 cups vegetable broth
- 1 cup diced onion
- 2 cloves garlic, minced
- 1 tsp ground coriander
- 1/2 cup heavy cream
- Salt and pepper to taste

Instructions:

1. In a large pot, sauté the onion and garlic until fragrant.
2. Add the parsnips, pears, coriander, and vegetable broth.
3. Bring to a boil, then reduce heat and simmer until parsnips are tender, about 20 minutes.
4. Puree the soup with an immersion blender until smooth.
5. Stir in the heavy cream.
6. Season with salt and pepper to taste and serve hot.

80. CHILLED CUCUMBER SOUP

Ingredients:

- 4 large cucumbers, peeled and chopped
- 2 cups plain yogurt
- 1 cup vegetable broth
- 1/2 cup fresh dill, chopped
- 2 cloves garlic, minced
- 1 tbsp lemon juice
- Salt and pepper to taste

Instructions:

1. In a blender, combine the cucumbers, yogurt, vegetable broth, dill, garlic, and lemon juice.
2. Blend until smooth.
3. Season with salt and pepper to taste.
4. Chill in the refrigerator for at least 2 hours before serving cold.

81. SWEET POTATO SOUP

Ingredients:

- 4 large sweet potatoes, peeled and chopped
- 4 cups vegetable broth
- 1 cup diced onion
- 2 cloves garlic, minced
- 1 tsp ground cumin
- 1/2 tsp ground cinnamon
- 1/2 cup coconut milk
- Salt and pepper to taste

Instructions:

1. In a large pot, sauté the onion and garlic until fragrant.
2. Add the sweet potatoes, cumin, cinnamon, and vegetable broth.
3. Bring to a boil, then reduce heat and simmer until sweet potatoes are tender, about 20 minutes.
4. Puree the soup with an immersion blender until smooth.
5. Stir in the coconut milk.
6. Season with salt and pepper to taste and serve hot.

82. TOMATO TORTILLA SOUP

Ingredients:

- 4 cups chicken broth
- 2 cups tomato sauce
- 1 cup diced onion
- 2 cloves garlic, minced
- 1 cup diced bell pepper
- 1 cup corn kernels
- 1 tsp ground cumin
- 1 tsp chili powder
- 1 cup shredded chicken (optional)
- Tortilla chips for garnish
- Shredded cheese for garnish
- Salt and pepper to taste

Instructions:

1. In a large pot, sauté the onion, garlic, and bell pepper until softened.
2. Add the chicken broth, tomato sauce, corn, cumin, and chili powder.
3. Bring to a boil, then reduce heat and simmer for 15 minutes.
4. Stir in the shredded chicken, if using.
5. Season with salt and pepper to taste.
6. Serve hot, garnished with tortilla chips and shredded cheese.

83. LEMON ORZO SOUP

Ingredients:

- 1 cup orzo pasta
- 4 cups chicken broth
- 1 cup diced carrots
- 1 cup diced celery
- 1 cup diced onion
- 2 cloves garlic, minced
- 1 lemon, juiced and zested
- 1 cup cooked shredded chicken
- 1 tsp dried thyme
- Salt and pepper to taste

Instructions:

1. In a large pot, sauté the onion, garlic, carrots, and celery until softened.
2. Add the chicken broth, thyme, and orzo pasta. Bring to a boil.
3. Reduce heat and simmer until orzo is tender, about 10 minutes.
4. Stir in the shredded chicken, lemon juice, and zest.
5. Season with salt and pepper to taste and serve hot.

84. GREEN BEAN SOUP

Ingredients:

- 1 lb fresh green beans, trimmed and chopped
- 4 cups chicken broth
- 1 cup diced potatoes
- 1 cup diced onion
- 2 cloves garlic, minced
- 1 cup diced tomatoes
- 1 tsp dried dill
- Salt and pepper to taste

Instructions:

1. In a large pot, sauté the onion and garlic until fragrant.
2. Add the chicken broth, potatoes, and green beans. Bring to a boil.
3. Reduce heat and simmer until vegetables are tender, about 20 minutes.
4. Stir in the diced tomatoes and dried dill.
5. Season with salt and pepper to taste and serve hot.

85. BARLEY AND VEGETABLE SOUP

Ingredients:

- 1 cup pearl barley
- 4 cups vegetable broth
- 1 cup diced carrots
- 1 cup diced celery
- 1 cup diced onion
- 2 cloves garlic, minced
- 1 cup diced tomatoes
- 1 tsp dried thyme
- Salt and pepper to taste

Instructions:

1. In a large pot, sauté the onion, garlic, carrots, and celery until softened.
2. Add the vegetable broth, barley, and thyme. Bring to a boil.
3. Reduce heat and simmer until barley is tender, about 30 minutes.
4. Stir in the diced tomatoes.
5. Season with salt and pepper to taste and serve hot.

86. GAZPACHO

Ingredients:

- 6 large tomatoes, chopped
- 1 cucumber, peeled and chopped
- 1 red bell pepper, chopped
- 1 green bell pepper, chopped
- 1 small red onion, chopped
- 2 cloves garlic, minced
- 3 cups tomato juice
- 1/4 cup olive oil
- 2 tbsp red wine vinegar
- Salt and pepper to taste
- Fresh basil or parsley for garnish

Instructions:

1. In a blender, combine the tomatoes, cucumber, bell peppers, onion, and garlic.
2. Blend until smooth.
3. Stir in the tomato juice, olive oil, and red wine vinegar.
4. Season with salt and pepper to taste.
5. Chill in the refrigerator for at least 2 hours before serving cold, garnished with fresh basil or parsley.

87. PUMPKIN BLACK BEAN SOUP

Ingredients:

- 1 can (15 oz) pumpkin puree
- 1 can (15 oz) black beans, drained and rinsed
- 4 cups vegetable broth
- 1 cup diced onion
- 2 cloves garlic, minced
- 1 tsp ground cumin
- 1/2 tsp ground cinnamon
- 1/4 tsp ground nutmeg
- 1/2 cup coconut milk
- Salt and pepper to taste

Instructions:

1. In a large pot, sauté the onion and garlic until fragrant.
2. Add the vegetable broth, pumpkin puree, black beans, cumin, cinnamon, and nutmeg.
3. Bring to a boil, then reduce heat and simmer for 20 minutes.
4. Stir in the coconut milk.
5. Season with salt and pepper to taste and serve hot.

88. SPINACH TORTELLINI SOUP

Ingredients:

- 1 package (9 oz) cheese tortellini

- 4 cups chicken broth
- 2 cups fresh spinach leaves
- 1 cup diced tomatoes
- 1 cup diced onion
- 2 cloves garlic, minced
- 1 tsp dried basil
- Salt and pepper to taste

Instructions:

1. In a large pot, sauté the onion and garlic until fragrant.
2. Add the chicken broth and bring to a boil.
3. Stir in the tortellini and cook until tender, about 7-9 minutes.
4. Add the diced tomatoes and spinach leaves.
5. Stir in the dried basil.
6. Season with salt and pepper to taste and serve hot.

89. Mushroom Spinach Soup

Ingredients:

- 1 lb mushrooms, sliced
- 4 cups vegetable broth
- 2 cups fresh spinach leaves
- 1 cup diced onion
- 2 cloves garlic, minced
- 1/2 cup heavy cream
- 1 tsp dried thyme
- Salt and pepper to taste

Instructions:

1. In a large pot, sauté the onion, garlic, and mushrooms until mushrooms are browned.
2. Add the vegetable broth and bring to a boil.
3. Reduce heat and simmer for 15 minutes.
4. Stir in the spinach leaves and heavy cream.
5. Add the dried thyme.
6. Season with salt and pepper to taste and serve hot.

90. CHICKEN TORTILLA SOUP

Ingredients:

- 1 lb chicken breast, cooked and shredded
- 4 cups chicken broth
- 1 cup diced tomatoes
- 1 cup corn kernels
- 1 cup diced bell pepper
- 1 cup diced onion
- 2 cloves garlic, minced
- 1 tsp ground cumin
- 1 tsp chili powder
- Tortilla strips for garnish
- Shredded cheese for garnish
- Salt and pepper to taste

Instructions:

1. In a large pot, sauté the onion, garlic, and bell pepper until softened.
2. Add the chicken broth, diced tomatoes, corn, cumin, and chili powder.
3. Bring to a boil, then reduce heat and simmer for 15 minutes.
4. Stir in the shredded chicken.
5. Season with salt and pepper to taste.
6. Serve hot, garnished with tortilla strips and shredded cheese.

91. CREAMY CELERY SOUP

Ingredients:

- 1 bunch celery, chopped
- 4 cups vegetable broth
- 1 cup diced onion
- 2 cloves garlic, minced
- 1 large potato, peeled and diced

- 1/2 cup heavy cream
- Salt and pepper to taste

Instructions:

1. In a large pot, sauté the onion and garlic until fragrant.
2. Add the chopped celery and diced potato, and sauté for another 5 minutes.
3. Add the vegetable broth and bring to a boil.
4. Reduce heat and simmer until the vegetables are tender, about 20 minutes.
5. Puree the soup with an immersion blender until smooth.
6. Stir in the heavy cream.
7. Season with salt and pepper to taste and serve hot.

92. SAUSAGE AND BEAN SOUP

Ingredients:

- 1 lb Italian sausage, sliced
- 4 cups chicken broth
- 1 can (15 oz) cannellini beans, drained and rinsed
- 1 can (15 oz) kidney beans, drained and rinsed
- 1 cup diced carrots
- 1 cup diced celery
- 1 cup diced onion
- 2 cloves garlic, minced
- 1 tsp dried thyme
- Salt and pepper to taste

Instructions:

1. In a large pot, cook the sausage until browned. Remove and set aside.
2. In the same pot, sauté the onion, garlic, carrots, and celery until softened.
3. Add the chicken broth, cannellini beans, kidney beans, and thyme.

4. Bring to a boil, then reduce heat and simmer for 15 minutes.
5. Stir in the cooked sausage.
6. Season with salt and pepper to taste and serve hot.

93. THREE BEAN SOUP

Ingredients:

- 1 can (15 oz) black beans, drained and rinsed
- 1 can (15 oz) kidney beans, drained and rinsed
- 1 can (15 oz) garbanzo beans, drained and rinsed
- 4 cups vegetable broth
- 1 cup diced tomatoes
- 1 cup diced onion
- 2 cloves garlic, minced
- 1 tsp ground cumin
- 1 tsp chili powder
- Salt and pepper to taste

Instructions:

1. In a large pot, sauté the onion and garlic until fragrant.
2. Add the vegetable broth, diced tomatoes, black beans, kidney beans, garbanzo beans, cumin, and chili powder.
3. Bring to a boil, then reduce heat and simmer for 15 minutes.
4. Season with salt and pepper to taste and serve hot.

94. SPINACH LEMON SOUP

Ingredients:

- 4 cups chicken broth
- 2 cups fresh spinach leaves
- 1 cup diced carrots
- 1 cup diced celery
- 1 cup diced onion
- 1/2 cup orzo pasta

- 1 lemon, juiced and zested
- 2 cloves garlic, minced
- Salt and pepper to taste

Instructions:

1. In a large pot, sauté the onion, garlic, carrots, and celery until softened.
2. Add the chicken broth and bring to a boil.
3. Stir in the orzo pasta and cook until tender, about 10 minutes.
4. Add the spinach leaves, lemon juice, and zest.
5. Season with salt and pepper to taste and serve hot.

95. DETOX BROCCOLI SOUP

Ingredients:

- 1 large head of broccoli, chopped
- 4 cups vegetable broth
- 1 cup diced onion
- 2 cloves garlic, minced
- 1 cup diced celery
- 1 cup diced carrots
- 1 tsp ground turmeric
- 1/2 cup coconut milk
- Salt and pepper to taste

Instructions:

1. In a large pot, sauté the onion, garlic, celery, and carrots until softened.
2. Add the chopped broccoli, turmeric, and vegetable broth.
3. Bring to a boil, then reduce heat and simmer until broccoli is tender, about 10 minutes.
4. Puree the soup with an immersion blender until smooth.
5. Stir in the coconut milk.
6. Season with salt and pepper to taste and serve hot.

96. BELL PEPPER AND LENTIL SOUP

Ingredients:

- 1 cup red lentils
- 4 cups vegetable broth
- 2 bell peppers, chopped
- 1 cup diced tomatoes
- 1 cup diced onion
- 2 cloves garlic, minced
- 1 tsp ground cumin
- 1 tsp smoked paprika
- Salt and pepper to taste

Instructions:

1. In a large pot, sauté the onion, garlic, and bell peppers until softened.
2. Add the vegetable broth, red lentils, diced tomatoes, cumin, and smoked paprika.
3. Bring to a boil, then reduce heat and simmer until lentils are tender, about 20 minutes.
4. Season with salt and pepper to taste and serve hot.

97. APPLE AND PARSNIP SOUP

Ingredients:

- 4 large parsnips, peeled and chopped
- 2 apples, peeled and chopped
- 4 cups vegetable broth
- 1 cup diced onion
- 2 cloves garlic, minced
- 1 tsp ground coriander
- 1/2 cup heavy cream
- Salt and pepper to taste

Instructions:

1. In a large pot, sauté the onion and garlic until fragrant.
2. Add the parsnips, apples, coriander, and vegetable broth.
3. Bring to a boil, then reduce heat and simmer until parsnips are tender, about 20 minutes.
4. Puree the soup with an immersion blender until smooth.
5. Stir in the heavy cream.
6. Season with salt and pepper to taste and serve hot.

98. BEET AND APPLE SOUP

Ingredients:

- 4 large beets, peeled and chopped
- 2 apples, peeled and chopped
- 4 cups vegetable broth
- 1 cup diced onion
- 2 cloves garlic, minced
- 1 tbsp lemon juice
- Salt and pepper to taste
- Sour cream for garnish

Instructions:

1. In a large pot, sauté the onion and garlic until fragrant.
2. Add the beets, apples, and vegetable broth.
3. Bring to a boil, then reduce heat and simmer until beets are tender, about 30 minutes.
4. Puree the soup with an immersion blender until smooth.
5. Stir in the lemon juice.
6. Season with salt and pepper to taste.
7. Serve hot, garnished with a dollop of sour cream.

99. CHICKEN BROCCOLI SOUP

Ingredients:

- 1 lb chicken breast, cooked and shredded
- 4 cups chicken broth
- 1 large head of broccoli, chopped
- 1 cup diced carrots
- 1 cup diced celery
- 1 cup diced onion
- 2 cloves garlic, minced
- 1/2 cup heavy cream
- Salt and pepper to taste

Instructions:

1. In a large pot, sauté the onion, garlic, carrots, and celery until softened.
2. Add the chicken broth and bring to a boil.
3. Stir in the broccoli and cook until tender, about 10 minutes.
4. Add the shredded chicken and heavy cream.
5. Season with salt and pepper to taste and serve hot.

100. SPINACH COCONUT SOUP

Ingredients:

- 4 cups vegetable broth
- 2 cups fresh spinach leaves
- 1 can (14 oz) coconut milk
- 1 cup diced onion
- 2 cloves garlic, minced
- 1 tbsp grated ginger
- 1 tbsp soy sauce
- 1 tsp ground turmeric
- Salt and pepper to taste

Instructions:

1. In a large pot, sauté the onion, garlic, and ginger until fragrant.

2. Add the vegetable broth, coconut milk, and turmeric. Bring to a boil.
3. Reduce heat and simmer for 10 minutes.
4. Stir in the spinach leaves and soy sauce.
5. Season with salt and pepper to taste and serve hot.

101. ARTICHOKE AND SPINACH SOUP

Ingredients:

- 1 can (14 oz) artichoke hearts, drained and chopped
- 4 cups vegetable broth
- 2 cups fresh spinach leaves
- 1 cup diced onion
- 2 cloves garlic, minced
- 1/2 cup heavy cream
- 1 tsp dried thyme
- Salt and pepper to taste

Instructions:

1. In a large pot, sauté the onion and garlic until fragrant.
2. Add the vegetable broth, artichoke hearts, and thyme.
3. Bring to a boil, then reduce heat and simmer for 10 minutes.
4. Stir in the spinach leaves and heavy cream.
5. Season with salt and pepper to taste and serve hot.

102. CREAMY CARROT SOUP

Ingredients:

- 1 lb carrots, peeled and chopped
- 4 cups vegetable broth
- 1 cup diced onion
- 2 cloves garlic, minced
- 1/2 cup heavy cream
- 1 tsp ground ginger

- Salt and pepper to taste

Instructions:

1. In a large pot, sauté the onion and garlic until fragrant.
2. Add the carrots, ginger, and vegetable broth.
3. Bring to a boil, then reduce heat and simmer until carrots are tender, about 20 minutes.
4. Puree the soup with an immersion blender until smooth.
5. Stir in the heavy cream.
6. Season with salt and pepper to taste and serve hot.

103. ROASTED GARLIC SOUP

Ingredients:

- 2 heads of garlic, roasted
- 4 cups chicken broth
- 1 cup diced onion
- 2 cloves garlic, minced
- 1/2 cup heavy cream
- 1 tsp dried thyme
- Salt and pepper to taste

Instructions:

1. Cut the tops off the heads of garlic, drizzle with olive oil, wrap in foil, and roast at 400°F (200°C) for 40 minutes.
2. In a large pot, sauté the onion and minced garlic until fragrant.
3. Squeeze the roasted garlic into the pot and add the chicken broth and thyme.
4. Bring to a boil, then reduce heat and simmer for 10 minutes.
5. Puree the soup with an immersion blender until smooth.
6. Stir in the heavy cream.
7. Season with salt and pepper to taste and serve hot.

104. BUTTERNUT PEAR SOUP

Ingredients:

- 1 large butternut squash, peeled and chopped
- 2 ripe pears, peeled and chopped
- 4 cups vegetable broth
- 1 cup diced onion
- 2 cloves garlic, minced
- 1/2 cup heavy cream
- 1 tsp ground cinnamon
- Salt and pepper to taste

Instructions:

1. In a large pot, sauté the onion and garlic until fragrant.
2. Add the butternut squash, pears, cinnamon, and vegetable broth.
3. Bring to a boil, then reduce heat and simmer until squash is tender, about 20 minutes.
4. Puree the soup with an immersion blender until smooth.
5. Stir in the heavy cream.
6. Season with salt and pepper to taste and serve hot.

105. CABBAGE DETOX SOUP

Ingredients:

- 1 small head of cabbage, chopped
- 4 cups vegetable broth
- 1 cup diced tomatoes
- 1 cup diced carrots
- 1 cup diced celery
- 1 cup diced onion
- 2 cloves garlic, minced
- 1 tsp ground turmeric
- 1 tsp ground ginger

- Salt and pepper to taste

Instructions:

1. In a large pot, sauté the onion, garlic, carrots, and celery until softened.
2. Add the cabbage, turmeric, ginger, and vegetable broth.
3. Bring to a boil, then reduce heat and simmer until vegetables are tender, about 20 minutes.
4. Stir in the diced tomatoes.
5. Season with salt and pepper to taste and serve hot.

106. TURMERIC LENTIL SOUP

Ingredients:

- 1 cup red lentils
- 4 cups vegetable broth
- 1 cup diced carrots
- 1 cup diced celery
- 1 cup diced onion
- 2 cloves garlic, minced
- 1 tsp ground turmeric
- 1 tsp ground cumin
- Salt and pepper to taste

Instructions:

1. In a large pot, sauté the onion, garlic, carrots, and celery until softened.
2. Add the vegetable broth, red lentils, turmeric, and cumin.
3. Bring to a boil, then reduce heat and simmer until lentils are tender, about 20 minutes.
4. Season with salt and pepper to taste and serve hot.

107. CARROT PARSNIP SOUP

Ingredients:

- 1 lb carrots, peeled and chopped
- 4 large parsnips, peeled and chopped
- 4 cups vegetable broth
- 1 cup diced onion
- 2 cloves garlic, minced
- 1/2 cup heavy cream
- 1 tsp ground coriander
- Salt and pepper to taste

Instructions:

1. In a large pot, sauté the onion and garlic until fragrant.
2. Add the carrots, parsnips, coriander, and vegetable broth.
3. Bring to a boil, then reduce heat and simmer until vegetables are tender, about 20 minutes.
4. Puree the soup with an immersion blender until smooth.
5. Stir in the heavy cream.
6. Season with salt and pepper to taste and serve hot.

108. CHICKEN ZOODLE SOUP

Ingredients:

- 1 lb chicken breast, cooked and shredded
- 4 cups chicken broth
- 2 large zucchinis, spiralized into noodles
- 1 cup diced carrots
- 1 cup diced celery
- 1 cup diced onion
- 2 cloves garlic, minced
- 1 tsp dried thyme
- Salt and pepper to taste

Instructions:

1. In a large pot, sauté the onion, garlic, carrots, and celery until softened.
2. Add the chicken broth and bring to a boil.
3. Stir in the shredded chicken and dried thyme.
4. Add the zucchini noodles (zoodles) and cook until tender, about 3-5 minutes.
5. Season with salt and pepper to taste and serve hot.

109. VEGAN CORN CHOWDER

Ingredients:

- 4 cups vegetable broth
- 3 cups corn kernels (fresh or frozen)
- 1 cup diced potatoes
- 1 cup diced celery
- 1 cup diced onion
- 2 cloves garlic, minced
- 1 cup coconut milk
- 1 tsp smoked paprika
- Salt and pepper to taste

Instructions:

1. In a large pot, sauté the onion, garlic, and celery until softened.
2. Add the vegetable broth, corn, potatoes, and smoked paprika.
3. Bring to a boil, then reduce heat and simmer until potatoes are tender, about 15 minutes.
4. Puree half of the soup with an immersion blender for a creamier texture.
5. Stir in the coconut milk.
6. Season with salt and pepper to taste and serve hot.

110. BLACK BEAN AND SWEET POTATO SOUP

Ingredients:

- 1 can (15 oz) black beans, drained and rinsed
- 1 large sweet potato, peeled and diced
- 4 cups vegetable broth
- 1 cup diced tomatoes
- 1 cup diced onion
- 2 cloves garlic, minced
- 1 tsp ground cumin
- 1 tsp chili powder
- Salt and pepper to taste

Instructions:

1. In a large pot, sauté the onion and garlic until fragrant.
2. Add the vegetable broth, sweet potato, black beans, diced tomatoes, cumin, and chili powder.
3. Bring to a boil, then reduce heat and simmer until sweet potatoes are tender, about 20 minutes.
4. Season with salt and pepper to taste and serve hot.

111. CREAMY ZUCCHINI SOUP

Ingredients:

- 4 large zucchinis, chopped
- 4 cups vegetable broth
- 1 cup diced onion
- 2 cloves garlic, minced
- 1/2 cup heavy cream
- 1 tsp dried basil
- Salt and pepper to taste

Instructions:

1. In a large pot, sauté the onion and garlic until fragrant.
2. Add the chopped zucchinis, basil, and vegetable broth.

3. Bring to a boil, then reduce heat and simmer until zucchinis are tender, about 15 minutes.
4. Puree the soup with an immersion blender until smooth.
5. Stir in the heavy cream.
6. Season with salt and pepper to taste and serve hot.

112. CARROT FENNEL SOUP

Ingredients:

- 1 lb carrots, peeled and chopped
- 1 large fennel bulb, chopped
- 4 cups vegetable broth
- 1 cup diced onion
- 2 cloves garlic, minced
- 1/2 cup heavy cream
- 1 tsp ground fennel seeds
- Salt and pepper to taste

Instructions:

1. In a large pot, sauté the onion, garlic, and fennel until softened.
2. Add the carrots, ground fennel seeds, and vegetable broth.
3. Bring to a boil, then reduce heat and simmer until carrots are tender, about 20 minutes.
4. Puree the soup with an immersion blender until smooth.
5. Stir in the heavy cream.
6. Season with salt and pepper to taste and serve hot.

113. CHICKPEA QUINOA SOUP

Ingredients:

- 1 can (15 oz) chickpeas, drained and rinsed
- 1/2 cup quinoa
- 4 cups vegetable broth

- 1 cup diced tomatoes
- 1 cup diced carrots
- 1 cup diced celery
- 1 cup diced onion
- 2 cloves garlic, minced
- 1 tsp ground cumin
- Salt and pepper to taste

Instructions:

1. In a large pot, sauté the onion, garlic, carrots, and celery until softened.
2. Add the vegetable broth, quinoa, chickpeas, diced tomatoes, and cumin.
3. Bring to a boil, then reduce heat and simmer until quinoa is cooked, about 15 minutes.
4. Season with salt and pepper to taste and serve hot.

114. POTATO CORN CHOWDER

Ingredients:

- 4 cups vegetable broth
- 2 cups corn kernels (fresh or frozen)
- 2 large potatoes, peeled and diced
- 1 cup diced celery
- 1 cup diced onion
- 2 cloves garlic, minced
- 1 cup heavy cream
- 1 tsp dried thyme
- Salt and pepper to taste

Instructions:

1. In a large pot, sauté the onion, garlic, and celery until softened.
2. Add the vegetable broth, potatoes, corn, and thyme.

3. Bring to a boil, then reduce heat and simmer until potatoes are tender, about 15 minutes.
4. Puree half of the soup with an immersion blender for a creamier texture.
5. Stir in the heavy cream.
6. Season with salt and pepper to taste and serve hot.

115. SPICY PEANUT SOUP

Ingredients:

- 4 cups vegetable broth
- 1 cup peanut butter
- 1 cup diced tomatoes
- 1 cup diced carrots
- 1 cup diced celery
- 1 cup diced onion
- 2 cloves garlic, minced
- 1 tsp ground cumin
- 1 tsp chili powder
- 1 tsp cayenne pepper (optional)
- Salt and pepper to taste

Instructions:

1. In a large pot, sauté the onion, garlic, carrots, and celery until softened.
2. Add the vegetable broth, diced tomatoes, peanut butter, cumin, chili powder, and cayenne pepper (if using).
3. Bring to a boil, then reduce heat and simmer for 15 minutes.
4. Stir well to combine all ingredients.
5. Season with salt and pepper to taste and serve hot.

116. GINGER CARROT SOUP

Ingredients:

- 1 lb carrots, peeled and chopped
- 4 cups vegetable broth
- 1 cup diced onion
- 2 cloves garlic, minced
- 2 tbsp grated fresh ginger
- 1/2 cup coconut milk
- Salt and pepper to taste

Instructions:

1. In a large pot, sauté the onion and garlic until fragrant.
2. Add the carrots, grated ginger, and vegetable broth.
3. Bring to a boil, then reduce heat and simmer until carrots are tender, about 20 minutes.
4. Puree the soup with an immersion blender until smooth.
5. Stir in the coconut milk.
6. Season with salt and pepper to taste and serve hot.

117. THAI GREEN CURRY SOUP

Ingredients:

- 4 cups vegetable broth
- 1 can (14 oz) coconut milk
- 1 cup diced carrots
- 1 cup diced bell peppers
- 1 cup diced onion
- 1 cup snow peas
- 2 cloves garlic, minced
- 2 tbsp green curry paste
- 1 tbsp grated ginger
- 1 tbsp soy sauce
- Fresh cilantro for garnish
- Salt and pepper to taste

Instructions:

1. In a large pot, sauté the onion, garlic, and grated ginger until fragrant.
2. Add the green curry paste and cook for another minute.
3. Add the vegetable broth, coconut milk, soy sauce, carrots, bell peppers, and snow peas.
4. Bring to a boil, then reduce heat and simmer until vegetables are tender, about 10 minutes.
5. Season with salt and pepper to taste.
6. Serve hot, garnished with fresh cilantro.

118. BUTTERNUT AND CARROT SOUP

Ingredients:

- 1 large butternut squash, peeled and chopped
- 1 lb carrots, peeled and chopped
- 4 cups vegetable broth
- 1 cup diced onion
- 2 cloves garlic, minced
- 1/2 cup heavy cream
- 1 tsp ground cinnamon
- Salt and pepper to taste

Instructions:

1. In a large pot, sauté the onion and garlic until fragrant.
2. Add the butternut squash, carrots, cinnamon, and vegetable broth.
3. Bring to a boil, then reduce heat and simmer until vegetables are tender, about 20 minutes.
4. Puree the soup with an immersion blender until smooth.
5. Stir in the heavy cream.
6. Season with salt and pepper to taste and serve hot.

119. RED BEAN SOUP

Ingredients:

- 1 can (15 oz) red beans, drained and rinsed
- 4 cups vegetable broth
- 1 cup diced tomatoes
- 1 cup diced carrots
- 1 cup diced celery
- 1 cup diced onion
- 2 cloves garlic, minced
- 1 tsp ground cumin
- 1 tsp smoked paprika
- Salt and pepper to taste

Instructions:

1. In a large pot, sauté the onion, garlic, carrots, and celery until softened.
2. Add the vegetable broth, red beans, diced tomatoes, cumin, and smoked paprika.
3. Bring to a boil, then reduce heat and simmer for 20 minutes.
4. Season with salt and pepper to taste and serve hot.

120. APPLE FENNEL SOUP

Ingredients:

- 4 large apples, peeled and chopped
- 1 large fennel bulb, chopped
- 4 cups vegetable broth
- 1 cup diced onion
- 2 cloves garlic, minced
- 1/2 cup heavy cream
- 1 tsp ground fennel seeds
- Salt and pepper to taste

Instructions:

1. In a large pot, sauté the onion, garlic, and fennel until softened.
2. Add the apples, ground fennel seeds, and vegetable broth.

3. Bring to a boil, then reduce heat and simmer until apples are tender, about 20 minutes.
4. Puree the soup with an immersion blender until smooth.
5. Stir in the heavy cream.
6. Season with salt and pepper to taste and serve hot.

121. ROASTED TOMATO SOUP

Ingredients:

- 4 cups cherry tomatoes
- 4 cups vegetable broth
- 1 cup diced onion
- 2 cloves garlic, minced
- 1/4 cup olive oil
- 1 tsp dried basil
- 1 tsp dried oregano
- Salt and pepper to taste

Instructions:

1. Preheat oven to 400°F (200°C).
2. Toss the cherry tomatoes with olive oil, salt, and pepper. Spread on a baking sheet and roast for 20 minutes.
3. In a large pot, sauté the onion and garlic until fragrant.
4. Add the roasted tomatoes, vegetable broth, basil, and oregano.
5. Bring to a boil, then reduce heat and simmer for 10 minutes.
6. Puree the soup with an immersion blender until smooth.
7. Season with salt and pepper to taste and serve hot.

122. ASPARAGUS SPINACH SOUP

Ingredients:

- 1 bunch asparagus, trimmed and chopped
- 4 cups vegetable broth

- 2 cups fresh spinach leaves
- 1 cup diced onion
- 2 cloves garlic, minced
- 1/2 cup heavy cream
- 1 tsp dried thyme
- Salt and pepper to taste

Instructions:

1. In a large pot, sauté the onion and garlic until fragrant.
2. Add the asparagus, thyme, and vegetable broth.
3. Bring to a boil, then reduce heat and simmer until asparagus is tender, about 10 minutes.
4. Add the spinach leaves and cook until wilted.
5. Puree the soup with an immersion blender until smooth.
6. Stir in the heavy cream.
7. Season with salt and pepper to taste and serve hot.

123. ROASTED VEGETABLE SOUP

Ingredients:

- 2 cups diced carrots
- 2 cups diced potatoes
- 2 cups diced bell peppers
- 1 cup diced onion
- 2 cloves garlic, minced
- 4 cups vegetable broth
- 1/4 cup olive oil
- 1 tsp dried thyme
- Salt and pepper to taste

Instructions:

1. Preheat oven to 400°F (200°C).
2. Toss the carrots, potatoes, bell peppers, onion, and garlic with olive oil, thyme, salt, and pepper. Spread on a baking sheet and roast for 25 minutes.

3. In a large pot, add the roasted vegetables and vegetable broth.
4. Bring to a boil, then reduce heat and simmer for 10 minutes.
5. Puree half of the soup with an immersion blender for a chunkier texture.
6. Season with salt and pepper to taste and serve hot.

124. CHICKPEA ORZO SOUP

Ingredients:

- 1 can (15 oz) chickpeas, drained and rinsed
- 1/2 cup orzo pasta
- 4 cups vegetable broth
- 1 cup diced tomatoes
- 1 cup diced carrots
- 1 cup diced celery
- 1 cup diced onion
- 2 cloves garlic, minced
- 1 tsp dried oregano
- Salt and pepper to taste

Instructions:

1. In a large pot, sauté the onion, garlic, carrots, and celery until softened.
2. Add the vegetable broth, diced tomatoes, chickpeas, and oregano.
3. Bring to a boil, then reduce heat and simmer for 10 minutes.
4. Add the orzo pasta and cook until tender, about 8-10 minutes.
5. Season with salt and pepper to taste and serve hot.

125. PUMPKIN LENTIL SOUP

Ingredients:

- 1 cup red lentils
- 4 cups vegetable broth
- 1 can (15 oz) pumpkin puree
- 1 cup diced carrots
- 1 cup diced onion
- 2 cloves garlic, minced
- 1 tsp ground cumin
- 1 tsp ground coriander
- 1/2 cup coconut milk
- Salt and pepper to taste

Instructions:

1. In a large pot, sauté the onion, garlic, and carrots until softened.
2. Add the vegetable broth, red lentils, pumpkin puree, cumin, and coriander.
3. Bring to a boil, then reduce heat and simmer until lentils are tender, about 20 minutes.
4. Stir in the coconut milk.
5. Season with salt and pepper to taste and serve hot.

126. TURMERIC CAULIFLOWER SOUP

Ingredients:

- 1 head of cauliflower, chopped
- 4 cups vegetable broth
- 1 cup diced onion
- 2 cloves garlic, minced
- 1 tbsp grated fresh ginger
- 1 tsp ground turmeric
- 1/2 cup coconut milk
- Salt and pepper to taste

Instructions:

1. In a large pot, sauté the onion, garlic, and grated ginger until fragrant.
2. Add the cauliflower, turmeric, and vegetable broth.
3. Bring to a boil, then reduce heat and simmer until cauliflower is tender, about 15 minutes.
4. Puree the soup with an immersion blender until smooth.
5. Stir in the coconut milk.
6. Season with salt and pepper to taste and serve hot.

127. SPINACH AVOCADO SOUP

Ingredients:

- 4 cups vegetable broth
- 2 ripe avocados, peeled and pitted
- 2 cups fresh spinach leaves
- 1 cup diced cucumber
- 1 cup diced onion
- 2 cloves garlic, minced
- 1 tbsp lime juice
- Salt and pepper to taste

Instructions:

1. In a blender, combine the vegetable broth, avocados, spinach leaves, cucumber, onion, garlic, and lime juice.
2. Blend until smooth.
3. Season with salt and pepper to taste.
4. Serve chilled or at room temperature.

128. TOMATO BASIL LENTIL SOUP

Ingredients:

- 1 cup red lentils
- 4 cups vegetable broth
- 1 can (15 oz) diced tomatoes

- 1 cup diced carrots
- 1 cup diced celery
- 1 cup diced onion
- 2 cloves garlic, minced
- 1/4 cup chopped fresh basil
- Salt and pepper to taste

Instructions:

1. In a large pot, sauté the onion, garlic, carrots, and celery until softened.
2. Add the vegetable broth, red lentils, and diced tomatoes.
3. Bring to a boil, then reduce heat and simmer until lentils are tender, about 20 minutes.
4. Stir in the chopped basil.
5. Season with salt and pepper to taste and serve hot.

129. SWEET POTATO KALE SOUP

Ingredients:

- 2 large sweet potatoes, peeled and diced
- 4 cups vegetable broth
- 2 cups chopped kale
- 1 cup diced onion
- 2 cloves garlic, minced
- 1 tsp ground cumin
- 1/2 cup coconut milk
- Salt and pepper to taste

Instructions:

1. In a large pot, sauté the onion and garlic until fragrant.
2. Add the sweet potatoes, cumin, and vegetable broth.
3. Bring to a boil, then reduce heat and simmer until sweet potatoes are tender, about 20 minutes.
4. Add the chopped kale and cook until wilted.
5. Stir in the coconut milk.

6. Season with salt and pepper to taste and serve hot.

130. Carrot Turmeric Soup

Ingredients:

- 1 lb carrots, peeled and chopped
- 4 cups vegetable broth
- 1 cup diced onion
- 2 cloves garlic, minced
- 1 tbsp grated fresh ginger
- 1 tsp ground turmeric
- 1/2 cup coconut milk
- Salt and pepper to taste

Instructions:

1. In a large pot, sauté the onion, garlic, and grated ginger until fragrant.
2. Add the carrots, turmeric, and vegetable broth.
3. Bring to a boil, then reduce heat and simmer until carrots are tender, about 20 minutes.
4. Puree the soup with an immersion blender until smooth.
5. Stir in the coconut milk.
6. Season with salt and pepper to taste and serve hot.

131. COCONUT CHICKPEA SOUP

Ingredients:

- 1 can (15 oz) chickpeas, drained and rinsed
- 4 cups vegetable broth
- 1 can (14 oz) coconut milk
- 1 cup diced tomatoes
- 1 cup diced carrots
- 1 cup diced onion
- 2 cloves garlic, minced
- 1 tbsp grated fresh ginger

- 1 tsp ground cumin
- 1 tsp ground coriander
- Salt and pepper to taste

Instructions:

1. In a large pot, sauté the onion, garlic, and grated ginger until fragrant.
2. Add the carrots, ground cumin, ground coriander, and vegetable broth.
3. Bring to a boil, then reduce heat and simmer until carrots are tender, about 15 minutes.
4. Add the chickpeas, diced tomatoes, and coconut milk.
5. Simmer for another 10 minutes.
6. Season with salt and pepper to taste and serve hot.

132. CHICKEN MISO SOUP

Ingredients:

- 1 lb boneless, skinless chicken breast, cut into bite-sized pieces
- 4 cups chicken broth
- 1/4 cup miso paste
- 1 cup diced tofu
- 1 cup sliced mushrooms
- 1 cup chopped green onions
- 1 cup chopped spinach
- 2 cloves garlic, minced
- 1 tbsp grated fresh ginger
- 2 tbsp soy sauce

Instructions:

1. In a large pot, bring the chicken broth to a boil.
2. Add the chicken pieces and cook until no longer pink, about 5 minutes.

3. Reduce heat to a simmer and add the mushrooms, garlic, and ginger.
4. Cook for 5 more minutes, then stir in the miso paste until dissolved.
5. Add the tofu, green onions, spinach, and soy sauce.
6. Simmer for another 5 minutes.
7. Serve hot.

133. LENTIL CARROT SOUP

Ingredients:

- 1 cup red lentils
- 4 cups vegetable broth
- 1 cup diced carrots
- 1 cup diced onion
- 2 cloves garlic, minced
- 1 tsp ground cumin
- 1 tsp ground coriander
- Salt and pepper to taste
- Fresh cilantro for garnish

Instructions:

1. In a large pot, sauté the onion and garlic until softened.
2. Add the carrots, ground cumin, ground coriander, and lentils.
3. Pour in the vegetable broth and bring to a boil.
4. Reduce heat and simmer until lentils and carrots are tender, about 20 minutes.
5. Season with salt and pepper to taste.
6. Garnish with fresh cilantro and serve hot.

134. BEET CARROT SOUP

Ingredients:

- 3 medium beets, peeled and chopped

- 4 cups vegetable broth
- 1 cup diced carrots
- 1 cup diced onion
- 2 cloves garlic, minced
- 1 tbsp grated fresh ginger
- 1/2 cup coconut milk
- Salt and pepper to taste

Instructions:

1. In a large pot, sauté the onion, garlic, and grated ginger until fragrant.
2. Add the beets, carrots, and vegetable broth.
3. Bring to a boil, then reduce heat and simmer until beets and carrots are tender, about 20 minutes.
4. Puree the soup with an immersion blender until smooth.
5. Stir in the coconut milk.
6. Season with salt and pepper to taste and serve hot.

135. GINGER BEET SOUP

Ingredients:

- 3 medium beets, peeled and chopped
- 4 cups vegetable broth
- 1 cup diced onion
- 2 cloves garlic, minced
- 1 tbsp grated fresh ginger
- 1/2 cup coconut milk
- Salt and pepper to taste

Instructions:

1. In a large pot, sauté the onion, garlic, and grated ginger until fragrant.
2. Add the beets and vegetable broth.
3. Bring to a boil, then reduce heat and simmer until beets are tender, about 20 minutes.

4. Puree the soup with an immersion blender until smooth.
5. Stir in the coconut milk.
6. Season with salt and pepper to taste and serve hot.

136. SWEET POTATO CHICKPEA SOUP

Ingredients:

- 1 can (15 oz) chickpeas, drained and rinsed
- 2 large sweet potatoes, peeled and diced
- 4 cups vegetable broth
- 1 cup diced onion
- 2 cloves garlic, minced
- 1 tsp ground cumin
- 1/2 cup coconut milk
- Salt and pepper to taste

Instructions:

1. In a large pot, sauté the onion and garlic until fragrant.
2. Add the sweet potatoes, ground cumin, and vegetable broth.
3. Bring to a boil, then reduce heat and simmer until sweet potatoes are tender, about 15 minutes.
4. Add the chickpeas and coconut milk.
5. Simmer for another 10 minutes.
6. Season with salt and pepper to taste and serve hot.

137. CREAMY COCONUT PUMPKIN SOUP

Ingredients:

- 1 can (15 oz) pumpkin puree
- 4 cups vegetable broth
- 1 cup diced onion
- 2 cloves garlic, minced

- 1 tbsp grated fresh ginger
- 1/2 cup coconut milk
- 1 tsp ground cumin
- 1 tsp ground coriander
- Salt and pepper to taste

Instructions:

1. In a large pot, sauté the onion, garlic, and grated ginger until fragrant.
2. Add the pumpkin puree, ground cumin, ground coriander, and vegetable broth.
3. Bring to a boil, then reduce heat and simmer for 10 minutes.
4. Stir in the coconut milk.
5. Season with salt and pepper to taste and serve hot.

138. LEMON SPINACH SOUP

Ingredients:

- 4 cups vegetable broth
- 2 cups fresh spinach leaves
- 1 cup diced onion
- 2 cloves garlic, minced
- 1/2 cup cooked rice or orzo
- 1 lemon, zested and juiced
- Salt and pepper to taste

Instructions:

1. In a large pot, sauté the onion and garlic until softened.
2. Add the vegetable broth and bring to a boil.
3. Reduce heat and add the fresh spinach leaves.
4. Cook until spinach is wilted, about 2 minutes.
5. Stir in the cooked rice or orzo, lemon zest, and lemon juice.
6. Season with salt and pepper to taste and serve hot.

139. BUTTERNUT RED PEPPER SOUP

Ingredients:

- 1 large butternut squash, peeled and chopped
- 2 red bell peppers, roasted and chopped
- 4 cups vegetable broth
- 1 cup diced onion
- 2 cloves garlic, minced
- 1/2 cup heavy cream
- 1 tsp ground cumin
- Salt and pepper to taste

Instructions:

1. In a large pot, sauté the onion and garlic until fragrant.
2. Add the butternut squash, roasted red peppers, ground cumin, and vegetable broth.
3. Bring to a boil, then reduce heat and simmer until vegetables are tender, about 20 minutes.
4. Puree the soup with an immersion blender until smooth.
5. Stir in the heavy cream.
6. Season with salt and pepper to taste and serve hot.

140. MUSHROOM QUINOA SOUP

Ingredients:

- 1 cup quinoa, rinsed
- 4 cups vegetable broth
- 2 cups sliced mushrooms
- 1 cup diced onion
- 2 cloves garlic, minced
- 1 tbsp soy sauce
- 1 tsp dried thyme
- Salt and pepper to taste

Instructions:

1. In a large pot, sauté the onion and garlic until fragrant.
2. Add the sliced mushrooms and cook until they release their juices.
3. Add the vegetable broth, quinoa, soy sauce, and dried thyme.
4. Bring to a boil, then reduce heat and simmer until quinoa is cooked, about 15 minutes.
5. Season with salt and pepper to taste and serve hot.

141. CREAMY PEA SOUP

Ingredients:

- 4 cups fresh or frozen peas
- 4 cups vegetable broth
- 1 cup diced onion
- 2 cloves garlic, minced
- 1/2 cup heavy cream
- Salt and pepper to taste
- Fresh mint leaves for garnish (optional)

Instructions:

1. In a large pot, sauté the onion and garlic until softened.
2. Add the peas and vegetable broth.
3. Bring to a boil, then reduce heat and simmer until peas are tender, about 10 minutes.
4. Puree the soup with an immersion blender until smooth.
5. Stir in the heavy cream.
6. Season with salt and pepper to taste and serve hot, garnished with fresh mint leaves if desired.

142. TOMATO CUCUMBER SOUP

Ingredients:

- 4 cups diced tomatoes
- 2 cups diced cucumbers
- 4 cups vegetable broth
- 1 cup diced onion
- 2 cloves garlic, minced
- 1 tbsp olive oil
- 1 tbsp red wine vinegar
- Salt and pepper to taste

Instructions:

1. In a large pot, sauté the onion and garlic in olive oil until softened.
2. Add the diced tomatoes, cucumbers, and vegetable broth.
3. Bring to a boil, then reduce heat and simmer for 10 minutes.
4. Stir in the red wine vinegar.
5. Season with salt and pepper to taste and serve hot or chilled.

143. SPINACH PUMPKIN SOUP

Ingredients:

- 1 can (15 oz) pumpkin puree
- 4 cups vegetable broth
- 2 cups fresh spinach leaves
- 1 cup diced onion
- 2 cloves garlic, minced
- 1/2 cup heavy cream
- Salt and pepper to taste

Instructions:

1. In a large pot, sauté the onion and garlic until softened.
2. Add the pumpkin puree and vegetable broth.
3. Bring to a boil, then reduce heat and simmer for 10 minutes.
4. Add the fresh spinach leaves and cook until wilted.
5. Puree the soup with an immersion blender until smooth.
6. Stir in the heavy cream.

7. Season with salt and pepper to taste and serve hot.

144. TOMATO BASIL QUINOA SOUP

Ingredients:

- 1 cup quinoa, rinsed
- 4 cups vegetable broth
- 2 cups diced tomatoes
- 1 cup diced onion
- 2 cloves garlic, minced
- 1/4 cup chopped fresh basil
- Salt and pepper to taste

Instructions:

1. In a large pot, sauté the onion and garlic until softened.
2. Add the diced tomatoes, quinoa, and vegetable broth.
3. Bring to a boil, then reduce heat and simmer until quinoa is cooked, about 15 minutes.
4. Stir in the chopped fresh basil.
5. Season with salt and pepper to taste and serve hot.

145. CARROT COCONUT SOUP

Ingredients:

- 1 lb carrots, peeled and chopped
- 4 cups vegetable broth
- 1 cup diced onion
- 2 cloves garlic, minced
- 1 tbsp grated fresh ginger
- 1/2 cup coconut milk
- 1 tsp ground turmeric
- Salt and pepper to taste

Instructions:

1. In a large pot, sauté the onion, garlic, and grated ginger until fragrant.
2. Add the carrots, turmeric, and vegetable broth.
3. Bring to a boil, then reduce heat and simmer until carrots are tender, about 20 minutes.
4. Puree the soup with an immersion blender until smooth.
5. Stir in the coconut milk.
6. Season with salt and pepper to taste and serve hot.

146. LENTIL SPINACH SOUP

Ingredients:

- 1 cup red lentils
- 4 cups vegetable broth
- 2 cups fresh spinach leaves
- 1 cup diced carrots
- 1 cup diced onion
- 2 cloves garlic, minced
- 1 tsp ground cumin
- Salt and pepper to taste

Instructions:

1. In a large pot, sauté the onion and garlic until softened.
2. Add the carrots, ground cumin, lentils, and vegetable broth.
3. Bring to a boil, then reduce heat and simmer until lentils and carrots are tender, about 20 minutes.
4. Add the fresh spinach leaves and cook until wilted.
5. Season with salt and pepper to taste and serve hot.

147. CAULIFLOWER COCONUT SOUP

Ingredients:

- 1 head of cauliflower, chopped
- 4 cups vegetable broth

- 1 cup diced onion
- 2 cloves garlic, minced
- 1 tbsp grated fresh ginger
- 1/2 cup coconut milk
- 1 tsp ground turmeric
- Salt and pepper to taste

Instructions:

1. In a large pot, sauté the onion, garlic, and grated ginger until fragrant.
2. Add the chopped cauliflower and ground turmeric, stirring to combine.
3. Pour in the vegetable broth and bring to a boil.
4. Reduce heat and simmer until the cauliflower is tender, about 15 minutes.
5. Puree the soup with an immersion blender until smooth.
6. Stir in the coconut milk.
7. Season with salt and pepper to taste.
8. Serve hot.

148. BEET LENTIL SOUP

Ingredients:

- 3 medium beets, peeled and chopped
- 1 cup red lentils
- 4 cups vegetable broth
- 1 cup diced onion
- 2 cloves garlic, minced
- 1 tbsp grated fresh ginger
- 1/2 cup coconut milk
- Salt and pepper to taste

Instructions:

1. In a large pot, sauté the onion, garlic, and grated ginger until fragrant.

2. Add the chopped beets and red lentils, stirring to combine.
3. Pour in the vegetable broth and bring to a boil.
4. Reduce heat and simmer until the beets and lentils are tender, about 20 minutes.
5. Puree the soup with an immersion blender until smooth.
6. Stir in the coconut milk.
7. Season with salt and pepper to taste.
8. Serve hot.

149. SWEET CORN AND PEA SOUP

Ingredients:

- 2 cups fresh or frozen corn
- 2 cups fresh or frozen peas
- 4 cups vegetable broth
- 1 cup diced onion
- 2 cloves garlic, minced
- 1/2 cup heavy cream
- Salt and pepper to taste

Instructions:

1. In a large pot, sauté the onion and garlic until softened.
2. Add the corn and peas, stirring to combine.
3. Pour in the vegetable broth and bring to a boil.
4. Reduce heat and simmer until the vegetables are tender, about 10 minutes.
5. Puree the soup with an immersion blender until smooth.
6. Stir in the heavy cream.
7. Season with salt and pepper to taste.
8. Serve hot.

150. TOMATO CHICKPEA SOUP

Ingredients:

- 1 can (15 oz) chickpeas, drained and rinsed
- 4 cups vegetable broth
- 2 cups diced tomatoes
- 1 cup diced onion
- 2 cloves garlic, minced
- 1 tsp ground cumin
- Salt and pepper to taste

Instructions:

1. In a large pot, sauté the onion and garlic until softened.
2. Add the diced tomatoes, chickpeas, and ground cumin, stirring to combine.
3. Pour in the vegetable broth and bring to a boil.
4. Reduce heat and simmer for 15 minutes.
5. Season with salt and pepper to taste.
6. Serve hot.

From Ani with love